RIGHTLY HANDLING
the WORD of TRUTH

Vic Reasoner

2120 Culverson Ave
Evansville, IN 47714-4811

TABLE of CONTENTS

The Word of Truth

Through the incarnation Jesus Christ, the living Word, became the God-man, fully God and fully man. To emphasize either side of this union, without maintaining the balance, is to fall into heresy. In a similar way the written Word has a dual nature. The Holy Spirit used fallible human agents to produce a sinless Savior and an errorless Scripture.

Liberals emphasize the human process and deny the supernatural source. Conservatives may assume that the Bible fell out of heaven and fail to appreciate the fact that God accommodated his revelation to human experience, language, culture, and literature. God revealed truth in ways we could grasp. John Calvin said in his comments on 1 Corinthians 2:7 that "He accommodates himself to our capacity in addressing us."[1]

We will examine both aspects — divine inspiration and human agency.

The Word of Truth is Divinely Inspired

We must grasp four basic concepts — revelation, inspiration, inerrancy, and authority.

---

[1]Calvin, *Commentary*, 20.1.104.

Revelation means unveiling. God has told us what we could otherwise not know. He is there and he has communicated in terms we can understand. God chose the most accurate method of communication. We got it in writing.

This revelation was sufficient, but not exhaustive. God has told us all we need to know. Where Scripture is silent, we must avoid the impulse to "fill in the blanks."

This revelation was progressive. God began with a skeleton and continued to add more flesh. Here liberalism imports the theory of evolution. This is not what is meant by *progressive*. It means God started us in the first grade teaching us the ABCs and then built upon that knowledge.

John Wesley exclaimed, "God himself has condescended to teach the way: for this very end he came from heaven. He hath written it down in a book. O give me that book! At any price give me the Book of God!"[2]

Inspiration means that God superintended the human authors, using their individual personalities, so that they composed and recorded without error his revelation to man. The purpose of inspiration is to insure infallibility.

The Bible claims divine inspiration

The Bible is called
- the oracles of God in Romans 3:2
- the Word of God in Luke 8:11
- the Word of the Lord in Acts 13:48
- the Word of Life in Philippians 2:16

---

[2]Wesley, *Preface* to Standard Sermons; *BE Works*, 1:105.

- the Word of Christ in Colossians 3:16
- the Word of truth in Ephesians 1:13
- the Word of faith in Romans 10:8

God said, *the Lord God said*, or *the Lord spoke saying* are phrases that occur 700 times in the Pentateuch; in the historical books 400 times.

Isaiah claimed his message came directly from God forty times, Jeremiah a hundred times, and Ezekiel sixty times. 2 Timothy 3:16 declares it was inspired by God. 2 Peter 1:21 explains the writers were moved by the Holy Spirit. These and similar statements declare over 2000 times that the Bible is the Word of God.

The New Testament quotes from nearly all of the 39 Old Testament books. Of the New Testament's 260 chapters, 209 chapters quote the Old Testament. Here are some examples of the regard the New Testament writers had for the Old Testament:

- Matthew 1:22 quotes Isaiah 7:14 as what the Lord has spoken
- In Matthew 19:5 Jesus quotes Genesis 2:24 as the words God said
- In Mark 7:9-13 the commandment of Moses is cited by Jesus as the word of God
- Luke 1:70 quotes from Zechariah as spoken by God through the prophets
- In Acts 2:16-17 the prophecy of Joel is quoted as what God says
- The Hebrew writer never gives credit to the human author except in 2:6 "someone said."

Inadequate explanations of inspiration

Inspiration is more than the author's intuition. The Bible gives information we could not know with certainty except through revelation. It is more than the illumination or spiritual perception we all may experience. It is more than a fallible record of human thought or religion. It is more than inspired concepts, but; the very words are chosen for a reason.

Inspiration Described

- Inspiration is Verbal

  You cannot dissect inspiration into substance and form. As for thoughts being inspired, apart from the words which give them expression, you might as well talk of a tune without notes, or a sum without figures. No such theory of inspiration is even intelligible. It is as illogical as it is worthless, and cannot be too sternly put down.[3]

- Inspiration is Plenary

  Plenary means full.

  By plenary inspiration, we mean that the whole and every part is divinely inspired. This does not necessarily presuppose the mechanical theory of inspiration, as some contend, or any par-

---

[3]Burgon, *Inspiration and Interpretation*, 120.

ticular method, only that the results of that inspiration give us the Holy Scriptures as the final and authoritative rule of faith in the Church.[4]

- Inspiration is Propositional

Propositional means truth which can be communicated in the form of a statement in which a predicate or object is affirmed or denied regarding a subject. Thus, it is open to verification. Truth is absolute. Truth is objective and thus open to verification. Truth is what corresponds to reality. All this is in opposition to existential, pragmatic, and subjective views of truth which are the presuppositions of liberal hermeneutics.

However, God not only spoke through propositions, but through attitudes, wishes, invitations, appeals, and reactions through his prophets. Sometimes he spoke through visions and signs, but basically through direct speech.

God's revelation is logical, following the conventional rules of grammar. God did not use nonsensical words which could only be understood by the initiated.

Inerrancy means free from error. This refers in accuracy in recording what was intended. God saw to it that his message was received without error. Some have said that God's activity in inspiration should be understood as parallel to his activity in salvation. Since God does not force salvation upon us, neither did he dictate nor control the human authors of Scripture.

But this comparison is misleading. While God does

---

[4]Wiley, *Christian Theology*, 1:183-184.

not unconditionally elect who will be saved, he has pre-destined the plan of salvation. While whosoever will may be saved, they will be saved on his terms — faith in the atoning work of his Son.

While the process of inspiration did not override the ability of the human authors to think, God revealed himself in and through their thinking.[5] The result was that these human authors accurately recording what God intended to reveal. This trustworthiness is claimed in such verses of Scripture as:

- In Psalm 12:6 *flawless* (טוהר - *tahor*) is used of pure gold without alloy. The emphasis here is on the final product. The statement that God's Word is like silver refined seven times expresses the concept of absolute purity or total freedom from imperfection. Seven was the number of completion or perfection.

- The process of refining gold is also used of God's Word in 2 Samuel 22:31, Psalm 18:30, 119:140, and Proverbs 30:5. *Flawless* (צרף - *tsarap*), used in all four of these references, means refined gold. What God says is completely reliable since it has been refined.

These metaphors borrow from the refining process and focus on the pure product. They are meant to convey the concept that all Scripture is without error.

- In Psalm 18:30 and 19:7 *perfect* means complete. The Hebrew adjective תמים (*tamim*) is also used of

---

[5]Frame, *The Doctrine of the Knowledge of God*, 29.

animals without blemish — "what is complete, entirely in accord with truth and fact."[6]

- Psalm 119:160 also declares that the whole of God's Word is truth and remains forever true.

- In Ecclesiastes 12:10 the author declares that what he wrote was upright and true.
- In Matthew 5:18 Jesus said the smallest letter or part of a letter would not have to be altered. Thus, inspiration is verbal, since God spoke by the mouth of all his prophets.

- Jesus said in John 17:17 that the Word of God is true.

- Jesus declared in Revelation 21:5 that his words are trustworthy and true. They did not lose those qualities in the process of John recording them.

Thus, John Wesley concluded:

Nay, if there be *any* mistakes in the Bible, there may as well be a thousand. If there be one falsehood in that book, it did not come from the God of truth.[7]

Wesley wrote a letter to the Bishop of Gloucester in response to the bishop's tract "On the Office and Opera-

---

[6]BDB, *Lexicon*, 1071.

[7]Wesley, *Journal*, 24 July 1776.

tions of the Holy Spirit." In it the bishop claimed that the Holy Spirit so directed the writers that "no considerable error should fall from them." Wesley objected to this language by writing, "Nay, will not the allowing there is any error in Scripture, shake the authority of the whole?"[8]

> No organism can be stronger than its weakest
> part, that if error be found in any one element,
> or in any class of statements, certainty as to any
> portion could rise no higher than belongs to that
> exercise of human reason to which it will be left
> to discriminate the infallible from the fallible.[9]

Yet a secretary could inerrantly recording the ravings of a madman and they would be worthless.

The **authority** of scripture is based simply on *who* inspired the book. Infallibility means it is trustworthy and reliable. God cannot lie (Titus 1:2). Jesus said in John 10:35 that Scripture cannot be broken. The Greek verb λύω (*luo*) means that is cannot be dissolved or contravened. Scripture cannot be annulled or its authority be defied because it is the Word of God. If God said it and the human authors got it down right, it is true and authoritative because of its source.

> There are four grand and powerful arguments
> which strongly induce us to believe that the Bi-
> ble must be from God; viz., miracles, prophecies,

---

[8]Wesley, *BE Works*, 11:504.

[9]Hodge and Warfield, "Inspiration," 242.

the goodness of the doctrine, and the moral character of the penmen. . . .

The Bible must be the invention either of good men or angels, bad men or devils, or of God.

1. It could not be the invention of good men or angels; for they neither would nor could make a book, and tell lies all the time they were writing it, saying, "Thus saith the Lord," when it was their own invention.

2. It could not be the invention of bad men or devils; for they would not make a book which commands all duty, forbids all sin, and condemns their souls to hell to all eternity.

3. Therefore, I draw this conclusion, that the Bible must be given by divine inspiration.[10]

Human Agency

Over a span of 1600 years, forty authors on three continents, used three languages to record God's revelation. God providentially ordered the life, education, and circumstances of each writer to fit him for his writing. They did not make any mistakes in any area; their memory was supernaturally aided.

Like an orchestra directed by the Spirit, each played a different part. This adaptation is like a man dictating to a PhD and to his small daughter, who puts the same message into different words which each can handle. The speech of Isaiah was florid and full; the message of

---

[10]Wesley, "Clear and Concise Demonstration of the Divine Inspiration of Holy Scripture," *Works*, Jackson, ed, 11:484.

Amos was plain and abrupt. Their personalities were not lost in the process.

Their sources of information include

- direct revelation. Daniel did not understand all of his vision (12:8-9).
- direct knowledge — they were often eyewitness. Yet Paul did not remember how many he had baptized (1 Cor 1:16)
- oral tradition
- short written accounts or notes
- personal contacts among writers
- ordinary sources of information; government documents. For example, much of Numbers is based on the results of a census. See

1 Kings 11:41; 14:29; 15:31
1 Chronicles 29:29
2 Chronicles 32:32; 36:23
Ezra 1:2-4; 4:7-23; 5:6-7; 6:6-12
Daniel 6:25-27

- Solomon and Luke did research according to 1 Kings 4:32-3; Luke 1:1-4. According to 1 Peter 1:10-11 the prophets *sought out* (ἐκζητέω - *ekzeteo*) or investigated and *searched out* (ἐξερευνάω - *exeraunao*) or investigated. These synonyms are both formed using the preposition εκ (*ek*) which means *out of* or *from*. This prefix intensifies the meaning to searching something out completely.

Yet at all times the biblical writers were superintended by Holy Spirit. However, John R. Rice taught that the entire Bible was verbally dictated by God.[11] While parts of Scripture definitely were, this theory does not take into account the variety of ways in which God conveyed truth. This makes the inspiration monolithic or uniform.

Variation in the Process of Inspiration

- God wrote the ten commandments himself (Deut 5:22).
- God dictated sections of Scripture.

The Old Testament records several instances of speech from God to individuals. God communicates to people by using actual spoken words, not simply communicating ideas or thoughts. Human language is not a barrier to effective communication by God.

Here are some examples of sections which God dictated directly:

Exodus 17:14; 24:4; 34:27
Numbers 33:2
Deuteronomy 31:22, 24
Joshua 24:26
1 Samuel 10:25
1 Chronicles 28:19
Jeremiah 1:9
1 Corinthians 2:13

Apparently the letters to the seven churches in Revelation 2-3 were dictated verbatim by the Lord Jesus.

---

[11]Rice, *Our God-Breathed Book*, 286.

Older theologians spoke of dictation referring to the fact that the authors wrote word for word what God intended, not that a particular method of stenography was necessarily used.

- God's words were spoken by prophets

A prophet is an authoritative messenger of God. *Thus says the Lord* was often used as the introductory formula of a royal decree. What the prophet says in God's name, God says. Sometimes an amanuensis took dictation from the prophet, such as Baruch did for Jeremiah (Jer 36:4).

- God's words written by a prophet

The prophets received supernatural information and spoke with prophetic utterance. According to Hebrews 1:1 revelation came at times by dreams or visions; in the case of Ezekiel it came by symbolic action and later by verbal communication.

Yet regardless of the variations in transmission, Peter said in 2 Peter 1:20 that Scripture did not arise from private self-inspiration, but that the prophets of old were carried along by the Spirit of God as wind in the sails moves a boat along the water. It is significant that Peter always used this verb φέρω (*phero*) in the passive voice except in 2:11, where it is used to explain what angels do *not* do.

This same verb occurred in 1 Peter 1:13, where it describes the glorification which Christ will bring at his revelation. This verb also occurs in 2 Peter 1:17-18, where the voice of the Father *was brought* to Christ and the apostles heard this declaration *brought* from heaven. In this context, *phero* describes revelation. But in v 21, where it occurs twice, it describes the process of inspiration. The word of God was never *revealed* by the will of man, but men spoke from God as they were *borne along* by the Holy Spirit.

Thus, in the immediate context of this chapter, where the verb occurs four times, the prophets and apostles somehow heard the voice of God declaring truth which could only be known through supernatural revelation, and they felt an obligation to somehow preserve and pass down this revelation. Eldon Fuhrman explained,

> Thus the divine initiative in producing Scripture was actualized by the determining and constraining influence of the Holy Spirit on select human agents. This is strong evidence for the plenary inspiration of the Holy Scriptures, and their entire trustworthiness as a result.[12]

Peter was not always infallible. In fact, Paul had to correct him according to Galatians 2:11-21. But when Peter was writing the Word of God, he was temporarily elevated to a state of infallibility through the Holy Spirit. Gleason Archer explained,

> As they wrote down God's revelation, the Old Testament authors were supernaturally born along (like sailing vessels impelled by the wind, *pheromenoi*) to record God's truth, which is not to be manipulated or perverted by one's own

---

[12]Fuhrman, *BBC*, 10:327.

personal interpretation or preference. Despite all the imperfections of the human writers of Scripture, the Lord was able to carry them along into his infallible truth without distortion or mistake.[13]

---

[13]Archer, "The Witness of the Bible," 95.

RIGHTLY HANDLING THE WORD OF TRUTH

Karl Barth said every theology stands or falls as a hermeneutic and every hermeneutic stands or falls as a theology.[14] While I believe Barth failed at both, he was right to see the connection.[15]

Evangelical theology first goes to the scripture to learn from it the doctrine of scripture, then in light of his pre-understanding he discerns in scripture principles of interpretation and he brings this set of principles to the scriptures to derive other doctrines.

Our exegesis, synthesis, and application is determined by a hermeneutic that is determined by an overall theology — a theology which rests on and supports itself by exegesis, synthesis, and application — also a spiral in the sense that we rise from a less exact and well-tested understanding to one that is more so. Systematic theology must be based on solid biblical exegesis and hermeneutics. Scripture must be interpreted by utilizing the rules of grammar and the facts of history. This leads to biblical theology, and biblical theology leads to a system-

---

[14]Packer, "Infallible Scripture and the Role of Hermeneutics. 325.

[15]Reasoner, "Karl Barth's Dialectic Doublespeak," 1-5.

atic theology. Through the inductive method, Scripture is first exegeted and then connected to form more general conclusions. Every relevant passage on a particular topic must be identified and a summary statement formulated which is consistent with all of the pertinent data. This process is sometimes described as the hermeneutical spiral or circle.

Methods of Interpretation

- Allegorical

This method regards the plain meaning of the words as merely a vehicle through which the deeper, more profound, mystical or spiritual meaning comes. The literal meaning is considered elementary and the hidden meaning is for the mature. The heathen toss eggs on a roof to see if they break or not, who read the entrails of chickens to determine their course of action are not much different from people who take a word of scripture out of context and then construct a subjective interpretation.

- It is subjective: each man is a law unto himself.
- It is rationalistic: Scripture is manipulated to suit man's reason.
- It obscures Scripture by imposing eisogesis for exegesis.
- It denies the historical situation of the text

Some of the rabbis fell into this approach to Scripture, such as Philo, a Hellenistic Jewish philosopher.

He was determined to get circuitously what he could not get directly. And thus did he practically create a Bible of his own — a Bible infinitely less venerable and more obscure — endowed with claims and interpreted by methods which were not derived from its own pages but were a feeble exotic transplanted from the theories of Greek philosophers into a completely alien soil.[16]

By the second and third centuries many of the church fathers used an allegorical approach to the Old Testament in order to find support for Christian doctrines. But even during early period there was opposition to allegorical exegesis from the School of Antioch in Syria.

According to A. Skevington Wood, the most valuable hermeneutical principle that Luther taught was his insistence on the literal or grammatico-historical sense.[17] Luther said that to allegorize is to juggle with Scripture. He said that the literal sense of Scripture alone is the whole essence of faith and of Christian theology. He rejected the Quadriga or fourfold hermeneutic of Scholasticism. Martin Luther declared,

I have observed that all the heresies and errors have arisen not from Scripture's own plain statements, but when that plainness of statement is ignored, and men follow the Scholastic

---

[16]Farrar, *History of Interpretation*, 131-136.

[17]Wood, *Luther and the Word*, 164.

arguments of their own brains.[18]

An Example of Allegory
Augustine on the Parable of the Good Samaritan

A certain man went down from Jerusalem to Jericho; Adam himself is meant; **Jerusalem** is the heavenly city of peace, from whose blessedness Adam fell; **Jericho** means the moon, and signifies our mortality, because it is born, waxes, wanes, and dies. **Thieves** are the devil and his angels. **Who stripped him**, namely, of his immortality; and **beat him**, by persuading him to sin; and **left him half-dead**, because in so far as man can understand and know God, he lives, but in so far as he is wasted and oppressed by sin, he is dead; he is therefore called, **half-dead**. The **priest** and **Levite** who saw him and passed by, signify the priesthood and the ministry of the Old Testament which could profit nothing for salvation. **Samaritan** means Guardian, and therefore the Lord Himself is signified by this name. The **binding of the wounds** is the restraint of sin. **Oil** is the comfort of the good hope; **wine** the exhortation to work with fervent spirit. The **beast** is the flesh in which he deigned to come to us. The **being** set upon the beast is belief in the incarnation of Christ. The **inn** is the church, where travelers returning to their heavenly country are

---

[18]Bornkamm, *Luther and the Old Testament*, 89.

refreshed after pilgrimage. The **morrow** is after the resurrection of the Lord. The **two pence** are either the two precepts of live, or the promise of this life and that which is to come. The **innkeeper** is the Apostle (Paul). The supererogatory payment is either his counsel of celibacy, or the fact that he worked with his own hands lest he should be a burden to any of the weaker brethren when the Gospel was new, though it was lawful for him "to live by the Gospel."[19]

However, there are some allegories in scripture. Paul specifically identifies Galatians 4:21-31 as an allegory (v 24). An allegory, in contrast to a parable, may establish several points of comparison. However, we must avoid the tendency to read into a passage what we want it to say. Augustine needed a catechism for new converts and misused this passage in order to fit his needs.
Philip Schaff explained,

The grammatico-historical exegesis is undoubtedly the only safe and sound basis for the understanding of the Scriptures as of any other book; and it is a wholesome check upon the wild licentiousness of the allegorizing method which often substitutes imposition for exposition.[20]

---

[19]Augustine, cited by Dodd, *Parables of the Kingdom*, 13-14.

[20]Schaff, *History of the Christian Church*, 2:816.

- Dogmatic

However, allegory was just as effective a tool in the hands of the heretic and the orthodox. Thus, Roman Catholic and Eastern Orthodox Churches accept the Bible as the first or primary authority along with the consensus of the early Fathers, the ecumenical creeds, and decisions of ecumenical councils, and oral tradition.

Thus, Scripture means what the Magisterium declares it means. The Magisterium is the official teaching authority of the Roman Catholic Church, consisting of the Pope and the bishops, which acts as the final, authoritative interpreter of the Word of God—comprising both Scripture and tradition.

This means the Roman Catholic Church alone can interpret Scripture, that the Church is the official interpreter of Scripture, and no passage of Scripture can be interpreted to conflict with Roman Catholic doctrine. For example, at the Council of Trent (1545-63) the Roman church ruled affirmed the doctrine of purgatory. They then adopted the apocryphal books which had a reference to purgatory and pronounced a curse on everyone who did not accept these books.

By the Middle Ages the prevalent approach to Bible interpretation held that the text had four levels of meaning. Of course, this approach had the effect of discouraging the non-professional from even reading, much less understanding the Bible. Thus, the Roman Catholic Church claims they alone can tell you what the Bible means. Their position is that Scripture and tradition have been deposited to the Roman Catholic Church and the responsibility for their interpretation lies with the Magisterium of the church, which they define as their own organization. According to Roman dogma, the pope when he speaks *ex cathedra* and the ecumenical councils are infallible. In reality, however, they have tended to misinterpret Scripture and elevate church dogma above Scripture. According to Gabriel Biel, a Roman Catholic theologian, "What the holy Church, our Mother, defines and accepts as catholic truth must be believed with the same reverence as though it were stated in Holy Scripture."[21]

Martin Luther resisted Roman Catholic dogmatism saying, "A layman who has Scripture is more than Pope or council without it."[22] Another time Luther objected, "I ask for Scriptures and Eck offers me the Fathers. I ask for the sun and he shows me his lanterns. I ask: 'Where is your Scripture proof?' and he adduces Ambrose and Cyril... With all due respect to the Fathers I prefer the authority of the Scripture."[23]

As Protestants we accept Scripture as our sole authority for faith and practice. John Wesley explained,

> The faith of the *Protestants*, in general, embraces only those truths, as necessary to salvation, which are clearly revealed in the oracles of God. Whatever is plainly declared in the Old and New Testaments is the object of their faith. They believe neither more nor less than what is manifestly contained in, and provable by, the Holy Scriptures. . . . The written Word is the

---

[21]Biel, *A Defense of Apostolic Obedience*, 75.

[22]Bainton, *Here I Stand*, 90.

[23]Farrar, *History of Interpretation*, 327

whole and sole rule of their faith, as well as practice. They believe whatsoever God has declared, and profess to do whatsoever He hath commanded. This is the proper faith of Protestants: by this they will abide, and no other.[24]

Wesley and the Reformers substituted an infallible Book for an infallible church.[25] In the late 1960s Albert Outler coined the phrase Wesleyan quadrilateral as a paradigm for the fourfold guidelines of authority in Wesleyan theology. It has been so widely misconstrued that Outler since expressed regret that he coined the term.

In its best sense it refers to the primacy of scriptural authority, complimented and corroborated by tradition, reason, and experience. However, if this is conceived geometrically the tendency would be to view all four as equal bases of authority. Instead of standing against the dual authority of Roman Catholicism, Wesleyanism is perceived as having four authorities!

- Mystical

Gnostic mysticism

Originally the mystical view of Scripture was based on Platonic philosophy which entered the church as gnosticism. On this basis Philo believed that hidden meaning lay behind numbers and names. For example, Genesis 2:10 describes a river which divides into four branches. Philo said this river was goodness, and it di-

---

[24]Wesley, "On Faith," Sermon #106, 1.8.

[25]Baker, "John Wesley's Churchmanship," 270.

vided into the four Greek virtues: prudence, temperance, courage, and justice.[26]

Pietistic mysticism

Much later in history, pietism emphasized the devotional aspects of Scripture. This was a reaction against mechanical and dogmatic exegesis, emphasizing the Bible as spiritual food. It tends to allegorize the Old Testament, discount doctrine, and emphasize an experience rather than doctrine. Is there a promise for me to claim? a duty to observe? an example to follow? a prayer to pray? a doctrine to accept? a principle to live by?

While this approach is a valid application, verses can be taken out of context to provide answers to personal dilemmas. Furthermore, there can be no objective verification of the existential interpretation. We should avoid opening the Bible at random in order to gain direction.

Admittedly, commentators can become dry and mechanical. The Word of God should be presented with life and anointing. The problem with the mystical interpretation is that it tends to reduce Scripture to only one dimension — that of personal spirituality. However, the Bible speaks to every sphere of life and its principles should produce a comprehensive world view influencing education, the arts, science and medical ethics, law and government.

The mystical approach is essentially an application, not an explanation. Before we can apply the text we must ascertain what it meant when it was written. The

---

[26]Klein, Blomber, and Hubbard, *Introduction to Biblical Interpretation*, 26.

abuses inherent within this approach are allegorizing, excessive typology, and neglect of prior doctrinal basis.

Secret Code Gnosticism

Michael Drosnin popularized the notion that there are secret messages encoded in Scripture.[27] In this cast the gnostics need computer technology to locate equidistant letter sequencing. This is also the thesis of Grant Jeffrey in *The Signature of God* (1996). Hal Lindsey believed this technology was referred to by Daniel, "Seal the words of the scroll until the time of the end" (12:4).[28] Actually this amounts to a high-tech version of divination which was forbidden in Scripture.

In *Hidden Prophecies in the Psalms*, J. R. Church also advocated the belief that there were cryptic messages in the Psalms which could only be discovered after 1948. Church argued that the first one hundred psalms corresponded to the hundred years of the twentieth century. He claimed that Psalm 48 foretold the formation of Israel as a nation in 1948. Since the book of Psalms was the nineteenth Old Testament book, when we add 19 to 1925 we get 1948. He also believed that since Psalm 88:10 described the rapture, the rapture would occur in 1988.[29]

Although there are a variety of occult systems of numerology, the most frequently used is the Jewish Kabbalah. This system takes certain letters of words

---

[27]Drossin, *The Bible Code* (1997).

[28]Hanegraaff, "Magic Apologetics," 54-55.

[29]Reasoner, "Hidden Prophecies in the Psalms?" 6.

(gematria) in a phrase and joins them together to for a new word with a hidden message.

Jonathan Cahn utilizes this Cabala or Kabbalah, beginning with *The Harbinger* (2011). Most forms of Kabbalah teach that every letter, word, number, and accent of scripture contains a hidden sense; and it teaches the methods of interpretation for ascertaining these occult meanings. These ancient mysteries are classic new age expressions which have been used for centuries by freemasonry, theosophy, and new age rabbis.

In the book of Colossians, Paul confronts a philosophy that was identified with the teachings of the Essenes. The apocalyptic tendencies of the Essenes distracted from the all-sufficiency of Christ. T. K Abbott wrote,

> The teaching of the Colossian false teachers was essentially traditional and esoteric. The Essenes, their spiritual predecessors, as well as the Gnostics, subsequently claimed to possess such a source of knowledge.[30]

According to Josephus, the Essenes required a secret oath before passing on their doctrines. So did the gnostics. The heresy which Paul addressed was a blend of Jewish and Greek elements.

While Cahn uses this Kabbalist method to find hidden meaning in the numerical arrangements of the Bible, this method may be applied to almost any piece of literature and draw almost any interpretation from it. Furthe-

---

[30]Abbott, *ICC*, 247.

rmore, the prophecy is always decoded *after* the fulfillment.

- Historical – Grammatical

This method advocates the natural, ordinary, usual sense of the words based on the laws of grammar and the facts of history. This is the usual way literature is interpreted. All secondary meanings depend upon previous objective literal sense. A large part of the Bible makes sense this way. This exercises a control on the imagination.

Karl A. G. Keil used the term *grammatico* which means the simple, direct, plain, ordinary, and literal sense of the phrases, clauses, and sentences. According to Kaiser, we usually mean *grammatical*, which deals more with syntax.[31]

Sentences involve grammar or syntax. In English the meaning of a sentence is often determined by the word order. However, "the rat ate the cheese" and "the cheese ate the rat" contain the same words but convey different meanings. In Greek the meaning is not determined by word order, but on word endings. Nouns and adjectives are declined and verbs are conjugated. The syntax of the sentence, as well as the definition of the words, determine the meaning. We begin translation by locating the main verb. It tells us five important facts:

- person – first, second, or third person
- number – singular or plural

------

[31]Terry, *Biblical Hermeneutics*, 203; Kaiser, *Toward An Exegetical Theology*, 87.

- voice – active, middle, or passive
- mood – indicative, subjunctive, optative, or impera-tive
- tense – present, imperfect, future, aorist, perfect, or pluperfect.

This means that nineteen variables are implied in the verb. Thus, recognition of Greek grammar goes a long way in eliminating subjective interpretations. A proposi-tional statement cannot legitimately mean anything I want to make it mean.

Defining Literal

Adam Clarke advised,

> Never take a text which you do not fully under-stand; and make it a point of conscience to give the *literal* meaning of it to the people: this is a matter of great and solemn importance. To give God's words a different meaning to what he intended to convey by them, or to put a construction upon them which we have not the fullest proof he has intended, is awful indeed![32]

Literal means the natural or usual construction, not the wooden literalism of extreme fundamentalism which makes the Bible a dead letter. Literalism must not be allowed to drift into a wooden letterism. 2 Corinthians 3:6 has been misemployed to pit the literal sense against

---

[32]Clarke, *Letter to a Preacher*, 101-102.

the spiritual sense. Literal is not opposed to spiritual and does not deny the use of symbolic language. We must distinguish between *literal* and *literalism*. While consistent literalism was the goal of dispensationalism, it was never attained.[33] However, liberalism objects to *literalism* on the basis that it wants to treat biblical accounts of certain events as myths or non-factual symbols.[34]

One dictionary definition says *literal* means taking words in their usual or most basic sense without metaphor or allegory. However, Robert Thomas, a classic dispensationalist, rejected "the extreme literal method" which "makes insufficient allowance for figures of speech in Scripture."[35] And John Shelby Spong claims it is heresy to read the Bible literally. Although he was an Episcopal bishop, he did not believe Jesus was the Savior of the world but he did ordain homosexuals. His argument against reading the Bible literally amounts to a false dilemma.

> So I am driven to find a different way to read the Bible that allows me simultaneously to be both a person of faith and a person thankful for and dedicated to the century in which I am privileged to live. For anyone to call the Bible the "Word of God" or to treat the words of the Bible as if they were words spoken by the mouth of God is to me not just irresponsible, it is also to

---

[33]Gentry, *The Great Tribulation*, 15.

[34]Packer, *"Fundamentalism" and the Word of God*, 104.

[35]Thomas, *Introduction to Exegesis*, 10.

be illiterate. To read from this book in a Sunday worship service and then to end that reading with some version of the phrase "this is the Word of the Lord" is, to me, little more than the perpetuation of religious ignorance and religious prejudice. . . .Yet I love this book. My life has been fed by this book, and I do not want to see it abandoned in an increasingly secular society. This is what drives me to search for an alternative way to read and to study the Bible. That is what compels me to go so deeply into this book that I can free it from the peril of literalism that has been imposed on it by well-meaning but uninformed "believers."[36]

Thus, defining *literal* can become confusing. Since the Bible contains genres which are naturally symbolic, the *literal* way to interpret them would be symbolic! In prophetic passages the symbols are to be understood as figurative because it is apparent from the context that they are symbolic.

It is an old and oft-repeated hermeneutical principle that words should be understood in their literal sense unless such literal interpretation involves a manifest contradiction or absurdity. It should be observed, however, that this principle, when reduced to practice, becomes simply an appeal to every man's rational judgment.[37]

---

[36]Spong, *Biblical Literalism*, 10-11.

[37]Terry, *Biblical Hermeneutics*, 247.

This literal approach means that we interpret the Bible according to the rules of grammar and the facts of history. It does not imply the disregard for symbolism, especially when it is apparent that the context is symbolic.

The task of the interpreter is to determine what the passage means and adhere rigidly to that meaning. This single sense amounts to the author's intended meaning. The primary task of the interpreter is to recognize the meaning which the author intended and to exegete the implications of that meaning.

According to James Rosscup, there are more than two hundred kinds of figurative language in Scripture.[38] This would include such literary devices as: simile, allegory, ellipsis, metaphor, paradox, irony, hyperbole, euphemism, personification, proverb, parable, and type.

Anthropomorphisms are not to be taken literally - God does not have a body but he adapted revelation to our limited understanding. However, he did not accommodate human error. Liberalism assumes that God adapted his revelation to the prevailing culture, accommodating their superstition, prejudice, and folklore. They then claim if God was inspiring writers today he might say the exact opposite since we have evolved.

As a young preacher I heard Paul Rees say that he did not take all of the Bible literally, but that he took it all seriously. Yet this methodology is consistent with a literal approach to Scripture! Thus, Bernard Ramm wrote,

The literal method of interpreting the Bible is to

---

[38]Rosscup, "Hermeneutics," 45..

accept as basic the literal rendering of the sentences unless by virtue of the nature of the sentence or phrase or clause within the sentence this is not possible. For example, figures of speech or fables or allegories do not admit of literal interpretation. The spirit of literal interpretation is that we should be satisfied with the literal meaning of a text unless very substantial reasons can be given for advancing beyond the literal meaning, and when *canons of control* are supplied.[39]

Carl Henry explained,

Like the man in the street and the scholar in ordinary conversation, the Bible uses everyday phenomenological language, as in references to the sun rising or setting. When Jesus referred to the size of the mustard seed, he had in mind neither twentieth-century scientific measurements nor a manual of the flora of Palestine; he was speaking in terms of his hearers' everyday experience.[40]

Wesley's hermeneutical presuppositions were identical with those of Luther and Calvin. Wesley wrote,

The general rule of interpreting Scripture is this: the literal sense of every text is to be taken,

---

[39]Ramm, *Protestant Biblical Interpretation*, 45.

[40]Henry, *God, Revelation and Authority*, 4:109.

if it be not contrary to some other texts. But in that case, the obscure text is to be interpreted by those which speak more plainly.[41]

Try all things by the written word, and let all bow down before it. You are in danger of [fanaticism] every hour, if you depart ever so little from Scripture; yea, or from the plain, literal meaning of an text, taken in connection with the context.[42]

Adam Clarke advised,

Never take a text which you do not fully understand; and make it a point of conscience to give the *literal* meaning of it to the people: this is a matter of great and solemn importance. To give God's words a different meaning to what he intended to convey by them, or to put a construction upon them which we have not the fullest proof he has intended, is awful indeed![43]

A Wesleyan Hermeneutic?

It is not valid to start the process of biblical interpretation with *a priori* assumptions that are unique to

---

[41]Wesley, Letter to Samuel Furly, 10 May 1755.

[42]Wesley, *BE Works*, 13:113.

[43]Clarke, *Letter to a Preacher*, 101-102.

Methodism. That is what concerns me about books such as *Reading the Bible in Wesleyan Ways*,[44] much of which goes against what Wesley taught, and *Reading Scripture as Wesleyans*. Joel Green wrote, "There are other ways to read the Bible, to be sure. But Methodists locate their reading of the Bible within the larger Wesleyan tradition. We read the Bible as Wesleyans." However, Green wants us to know that being Wesleyan is "not in the sense of marching lockstep to his cadence or matching his gait with our own."[45]

It should come as no surprise that if I approach Scripture with certain presuppositions, I will find confirmation for what I assume to be in Scripture. But if every theological tradition follows suit, the result is that no one can agree on what the Bible actually says. If Scripture is our final authority and we approach Scripture with a commitment to inductive study, we may find that we have broad agreement that extends beyond our own tradition.

The grammatical-historical hermeneutic is not only the most objective and inductive method, it is also the broad Reformation and Protestant hermeneutic. However, a new generation of "Wesleyan" scholars is trying to establish credibility by capitulating to the old liberalism. For these new "Wesleyans," nothing the Bible records can be regarded as accurate historically unless it is confirmed independently. In so doing they have implicitly denied the authority of Scripture. Yet pagan and

---

[44]Callen and Thompson, *Reading the Bible in Wesleyan Ways* (2004).

[45]Green, *Reading Scripture as Wesleyans*, ix-x.

secular history is often nothing more than propaganda. A safer position would be not to accept any historical claims which contradict Scripture.

Steven Koskie explained the process of employing a "Wesleyan hermeneutic." The first step is to read Wesley's writings to see how he approached Scripture. However, the meaning is not to be found within the biblical text, but as a result of the reader, the text, and the context. Thus, hermeneutics has been redefined as a subjective meaning which the reader gets from the text. But a reader-response hermeneutic is audience or reader-centered. Readers often interpret the same text differently. Thus, the *Global Wesleyan Encyclopedia of Biblical Theology* contains entries on no less than twelve different hermeneutical approaches, such as African, Asian, Canonical, Caribbean, Feminist, Indian, Intertextuality, Latin American, Missional, Reader-Response, Theological, and Wesleyan.

The methodology Wesley employed and themes he emphasized then become the lens through which Scripture is read. However, this Wesleyan reading of Scripture has adopted Wesley as the starting point. I would argue that Wesley must be read in light of the Scripture and not that the Scripture is to be read in light of Wesley. It is also significant that Wesley himself did not interpret the Bible this way, nor could he. He had to begin with something prior to himself. Wesley wrote, "We believe the written word of God to be the *only and the sufficient* rule both of Christian faith and practice."[46]

And so why arbitrarily start with Wesley? We must start with Scripture itself. Every interpreter amounts to

---

[46]Wesley, *BE Works*, 9:34.

a different voice and the church in unable to speak with one voice if we start with the interpreter. The result is that we can discuss what the Bible means only with those who read it through our lens. This new approach is actually based on postmodern presuppositions that there is no one unifying, overarching meta-narrative. The result is we only see what we look for and we never see the whole picture.

Koskie even conceded that a Wesleyan hermeneutic might even vary between different Wesleyan traditions. Yet he assures us that the text cannot mean just anything. There are parameters, which apparently are established by the reader. He explained that this was a "ruled reading." These rules are established by the "context" in which the reader reads. Apparently the individual reader approaches the text within an established context or hermeneutical tradition.[47] But how do we know which hermeneutical tradition is correct?

Even if we accept the assumption of a unique and sectarian "Wesleyan hermeneutic," such a hermeneutic should not presuppose liberal assumptions. Joel Green seems to imply that a Wesleyan hermeneutic would accept higher criticism, but would be more focused on soteriological themes. Those who advocate a "Wesleyan hermeneutic" seem to be implying that we should embrace the theology of Karl Barth, while still claiming to read through the lens of Wesley.

Thomas Oden wrote that Wesley followed Luther and Calvin in their method in reading Scripture texts.[48]

---

[47]Koskie, "Wesleyan Hermeneutics," 395-401.

[48]Oden, *John Wesley's Teachings*, 1:71.

Prior to the Reformation the Roman church determined what the Bible meant. Beginning at the time of the Protestant Reformation, theologians had to wrestle with the proper hermeneutical method. Wesley wrote,

> The general rule of interpreting Scripture is this: the literal sense of every text is to be taken, if it be not contrary to some other texts. But in that case, the obscure text is to be interpreted by those which speak more plainly.[49]

Wesley also warned,

> Try all things by the written Word, and let all bow down before it. You are in danger of [fanaticism] every hour, if you depart ever so little from Scripture; yea, or from the plain, literal meaning of any text, taken in connection with the context.[50]

According to Albert Outler, Wesley had five principles of biblical interpretation.

- Believers should become accustomed to the general sense of the Bible as a whole.
- Obscure texts should be illuminated by clearer texts. "There is no authority above Scripture from which a more definitive interpretation of revelation may be sought."

---

[49]Wesley, *Letter* to Samuel Furly, 10 May 1755.

[50]Wesley, *BE Works*, 13:113.

- The literal sense should guide us unless it leads to conclusions which are irrational or unworthy of God's moral character. Any other interpretation must be compatible with the analogy of faith or the general themes of Scripture. Thus, to claim that Wesley's hermeneutic was *love* is reductionary [51]
- All moral commands in Scripture are "covered promises," since God never commands the impossible and his grace is always sufficient.
- The traditional interpretation within the historic Christian church, while fallible, is more likely the better interpretation.[52] This is a restatement of the position articulated by Vincent of Lérins of the fifth century.

Wesley advocated setting apart time every morning and evening, reading a chapter out of the Old and New Testaments, reading with a single eye to know the whole will of God, keeping in mind the analogy of faith, the connection and harmony between fundamental doctrine, serious and earnest prayer for understanding, and frequent pauses to examine ourselves.[53]

Thorsen wrote that Wesley also utilized deductive reasoning. In fact, the deductive approach was predominate in all his writings. Thus, he approached Scripture believing it to be entirely trustworthy and proceeded logically from general to specific truths.

According to Thorsen, Wesley began by studying the

---

[51]Wynkoop, "Hermeneutical Approach to John Wesley," 21.

[52]Outler, "Introduction," *BE Works of John Wesley*, 1:58-59.

[53]Wesley, *Notes*, 1:1.

text, relying also upon experience. "Of course, Wesley did *not* expect experience ever to contradict Scripture." Along with experience, reason played a vital role. Wesley also considered the leadership of the Holy Spirit consistent with our rational capabilities.[54]

Therefore, if we use the same hermeneutic that Wesley used, we will employ the grammatical-historical hermeneutic which was common to all the Protestant Reformers.

- Historical – Critical

In the *Wesleyan Theological Journal*, George Lyons wrote "Hermeneutical Bases for Theology: Higher Criticism and the Wesleyan Interpreter." Lyons argues that since Wesley incorporated the contemporary biblical criticism of his day, he should serve as an example for us, and Wesleyan interpreters today must become familiar with the current methods, results, and practice of higher criticism. Lyons conceded that "we cannot uncritically swallow all its naturalistic and rationalistic assumptions, but neither can we ignore its more numerous values."[55] This "pied piper" tune was also played by Milton S. Terry.[56]

However, Lyons is misleading. John Wesley was abreast with current developments in biblical scholar-

---

[54]Thorsen, *The Wesleyan Quadrilateral,* 143-147.

[55]Lyons, "Hermeneutical Bases for Theology," 73.

[56]See my forthcoming book: *Milton S. Terry: A Theological Biography as a Trajectory of American Methodism: Lessons Not Learned.*

ship, but did not necessarily adopt them. A. Skevington Wood said that while it is fashionable to dismiss Wesley's conservative approach to Scripture saying that he lived in pre-critical times and had been living today would have adopted more liberal views, fails to take into account that Wesley was conscious of the beginning of the development of higher criticism — yet did not embrace it. Wood listed Richard Simon, Jean Astrue, Charles Boyle, and Richard Bently, all as critics with whom Wesley would have been familiar.[57]

George Allen Turner wrote, "To classify Wesley as a 'critical' scholar represents a vain attempt to 'modernize' him."[58]

Robert Coleman explained,

> Some have said that his biblicism was because he lived in a pre-critical age. But this was not the case. Views questioning biblical integrity were beginning to circulate in Europe in the latter part of the eighteenth century. Wesley simply had no use for them. He gave no credence to scholars who stood in judgment upon the oracles of God.[59]

Wesley was not impressed with the critics of his day. He wrote,

> It would be excusable if these menders of the

---

[57]Wood, *The Burning Heart*, 217-218.

[58]Turner, "John Wesley as an Interpreter of Scripture," 162.

[59]Coleman, *"Nothing to Do But to Save Souls,"* 29-30.

Bible would offer their hypotheses *modestly*. But one cannot excuse them when they not only obtrude their novel scheme, with the *utmost confidence*, but even *ridicule* that scriptural one which always was and is now held by men of the greatest learning and piety in the world. Hereby they promote the cause of infidelity more effectually than either Hume or Voltaire.[60]

The origin and spread of higher criticism

In the seventeenth century, German secular universities approached Scripture with a rationalistic attitude. They taught the universe is ruled by set laws which cannot be suspended or altered and therefore miracles were impossible. The idea that God spoke or intervened was dismissed. Thus, the Bible was analyzed solely as human literature. There was no divine inspiration.

Higher criticism is rationalistic and uses selective data. Evolutionary concepts are imposed upon the religion of Israel. Inspiration and the supernatural are both redefined.

Julius Wellhausen (1844-1918) developed an elaborate system of sources for the Pentateuch. This "cut and paste" approach to the Scriptures produced the documentary hypothesis which explained the five books of Moses were actually written by four different sources and later pieced together into its present form a thousand years after Moses. Thus the Pentateuch is not regarded as historically accurate, but a natural product of

---

[60]Wesley, *Journal*, 8 August 1773.

the Jewish religion.

F. C. Baur (1792-1860) handled the New Testament in a similar way. Baur saw Peter and Paul as antagonistic to one another in their writings. Baur believed that the second century church wrote most of the New Testament, which were doctored, and that these writings differed greatly from the historical Jesus.

In the eighteenth century science adopted Enlightenment philosophy which categorically ruled out the possibility of miracles. They sought a natural explanation for all things and exchanged their belief in a Creator God for the theory of evolution. For the first time science was pitted against scripture and historic Christianity was perceived as behind the times.

Until the nineteenth century, it was left to infidels outside the church to question the integrity of the Scriptures. The Word of God claimed to be inspired by God and the message of the Bible was internally consistent with that claim. This divine inspiration was confirmed by fulfilled prophecy and by miracles. The church recognized the same Scriptures as did the Jewish religion, plus the writings of the apostles were also recognized as being authoritative and were placed on an equal basis with the Old Testament Scriptures.

In an effort to reconcile science and Scripture, liberal theologians tended to reinterpret Scripture in the light of scientific theory. Instead of concentrating on the biblical text, the trend was to develop naturalistic theories as to how the text came into being.

The massive, twelve-volume *Cyclopedia of Biblical, Theological, and Ecclesiastical Literature*, published between 1867-1887, did not initially have an article on Bible Criticism. However, at the end of the second volume and out of alphabetical order, a two-page supplementary article on criticism is inserted. I believe this demonstrates the point in time when continental liberalism began to influence American theology.

When Hinckley G. Mitchell of Boston University School of Theology questioned the Mosaic authorship of the Pentateuch, the Methodist bishops brought charges against him in 1896. He was not convicted of heresy. However, the issue flared up again in 1900 and in 1905 his appointment was not renewed.[61]

In Britain the Methodists were the most consistently conservative on Scripture and acceptance of the new criticism came more slowly than among the Baptists, Congregationalists, or Presbyterians in the decades before World War I. Wesley had promoted in Britain both a learned study of the Bible and an intense interest in the Spirit. Evangelicals were not forced to choose between the two.

Methodism was about a quarter of a century behind the general biblical higher criticism controversy. Higher criticism was opposed as early as 1856 in the Wesleyan Methodist Magazine, by editor William L. Thornton. He was succeeded by Benjamin Gregory who was even more militant. The magazine also opposed evolution calling it "exceedingly fanciful and unsubstantiated" in 1867.[62]

Charles H. Fowler, an American Methodist bishop, said, "It may seem a severe thing for a Methodist bishop, and one who has been president of one of our largest

---

[61]Brown, "Higher Criticism Comes to America," 205. See also Munhall, *Breakers! Methodism Adrift*, 13, 72-83.

[62]Dunlap, "Methodist Theology in Great Britain," 426-441.

universities to say, but nevertheless I believe it to be true that the schools and universities of the Methodist Episcopal Church belong more to the devil to-day than they do to our Church."[63]

In 1963 Robert Brush, a founder of the Fundamental Wesleyan Society, traveled to Marion, Indiana to express his concerns over the influence of higher criticism in Wesleyan Sunday School literature. Our concerns were ignored and the situation has not improved.

Subsequent humanistic criticism

- Source criticism

Source criticism assumed that Matthew, Mark, Luke, and John did not actually write the gospels which bear their names. Instead, eyewitness accounts were passed on orally for a generation. Some were embellished or modified over the passage of time. Then these eyewitness accounts were gathered, edited, and written down in a document called Quelle or Q. None of the critics have ever seen this document called Q, but it is assumed that the editors who compiled Matthew, Mark, and Luke all drew from this source and altered the material to address needs within the early church. Thus the higher critics had more faith in a Q document they have never seen than in the Word of God which they held in their hands.

- Form criticism

---

[63]quoted by Munhall, *Breakers*, 64.

After source criticism fragmented the entire Bible, form criticism built upon this unproven assumption. Form criticism, which dominated scholarship in the first half of the twentieth century, attempted to reconstruct each independent unit between the oral traditions and the written Word of God as we now have it. It was assumed that the church created legends, tales, myths, and parables to meet particular needs which existed at the time. This places the church in authority over the Word since the word of God was claimed to have been carried orally before the church wrote it down. What is overlooked is that the authority is not vested in who wrote it down, but who spoke it!

The Bible was regarded as a piece of propaganda created by the church to serve its own interests. They emphasize the *sitz in laben* or the life situation that produced writing. It is legitimate to consider the culture and circumstances surrounding the writing *so long as we do not conclude that the inspired account was fabricated or embellished to serve a certain purpose.* Liberals always forget that part of the life situation which produced the writing was the inspiration of the Holy Spirit.

Rudolf Bultmann, one of the most famous form critics, attempted to strip away the mythology that he claimed had developed about Jesus and when Bultmann had finished he ended up with only forty brief sayings he considered genuine. The myth was considered a vehicle for expressing the reality. The ideal is transcendent and must be abstracted from the text. In 1961 Bultmann declared,

It is impossible to use electric light and the wireless [radio] and to avail ourselves of modern medical and surgical discoveries, and at the same time to believe in the New Testament world of demons and spirits.[64]

Eta Linnemann, a student of Bultmann, estimates that historical-critical theology assumes upwards of 80-90% of the hypotheses without verification.[65] Thus, the historical-critical method is an *a priori* approach to locate the canon in the canon, which will produce a historical-critical interpretation as to what constitutes the canon.[66]

It seems however that only a certified form critic is capable of discerning the *sitz en laben*. C. S. Lewis, who was an authority in medieval literature, expressed his skepticism with biblical criticism:

1. These men ask me to believe they can read between the lines of the old texts; the evidence is their obvious inability to read (in any sense worth discussing) the lines themselves. They claim to see fern-seed and can't see an elephant ten yards away in broad daylight. . . .

2. All theology of the liberal type involves at some point — and often involves throughout —

---

[64]Bultmann, "New Testament and Mythology." 5.

[65]Linnemann, *Historical Criticism of the Bible*, 96. See also Linnemann, *Biblical Criticism on Trial*, 177-188.

[66]Maier, *End of the Historical-Critical Method*, 9-11.

the claim that the real behavior and purpose
and teaching of Christ came very rapidly to be
misunderstood and misrepresented by His fol-
lowers, and has been recovered or exhumed only
by modern scholars. . . .

3. I find in these theologians a constant use of
the principle that the miraculous does not occur.
. . . I only want to point out that this is a purely
philosophical question. Scholars, as scholars,
speak on it with no more authority than anyone
else. . . . On this they speak simply as men; men
obviously influenced by, and perhaps insuffi-
ciently critical of, the spirit of the age they grew
up in.

4. All this sort of criticism attempts to reconstruct the genesis of the texts it studies; what
vanished documents each author used, when
and where he wrote, with what purposes, under
what influences — the whole *Sitz im Leben* of
the text. This is done with immense erudition
and great ingenuity. And at first sight it is very
convincing. . . . What forearms me against all
these Reconstructions is the fact that I have
seen it all from the other end of the stick. I have
watched reviewers reconstruction the genesis of
my own books in just this way. Until you come to
be reviewed yourself you would never believe
how little of an ordinary review is taken up by
criticism in the strict sense: by evaluation,
praise, or censure, of the book actually written.
Most of it is taken up with imaginary histories of

the process by which you wrote it. . . . Reviewers, both friendly and hostile, will dash you off such histories with great confidence; will tell you what public events had directed the author's mind to this or that, what other authors had influenced him, what his over-all intention was, what sort of audience he principally addressed, why — and when — he did everything. . . . My impression is that in the whole of my experience not one of these guesses has on any one point been right; that the method shows a record of 100 per cent failure. . . . Dr. Bultmann never wrote a gospel. Has the experience of his learned, specialized, and no doubt meritorious, life really given him any power of seeing into the minds of those long dead men who were caught up into what, on any view, much be regarded as the central religious experience of the whole human race? It is no incivility to say — he himself would admit — that he must in every way be divided from the evangelists by far more formidable barriers — spiritual as well as intellectual — than any that could exist between my reviewers and me.[67]

• Redaction Criticism

The next theory to gain popularity was redaction criticism — a term coined by Willi Marxsen in 1954. The focus moved to the redactors or editors who picked and chose what material would be interwoven to create the

---

[67]Lewis, *Fern-seed*, 111-118.

biblical accounts and what motivated these editors to select the material which we now have. This is like playing Jeopardy — you are given the answer and have to deduce the question. This draws the interpreter away from the text to guessing what motivated the editor. This approach can only be used where similar documents can be compared. Thus redaction criticism operates primarily in the Gospel accounts and in the Old Testament between Samuel, Kings, and Chronicles. It is assumed that different church situations produced different accounts.

There may be literary dependance, but in humility we could never announce that fact with complete certainty. However, once again redaction criticism gives very little input in terms of the meaning of the final text. While there was selectivity and arrangement of events by gospel writers, there was not modification and creativity.

Midrash is a literary genre which allows for embellishment — a mixture of historical literature and fabrication to prove or emphasize a particular point. The Talmud, a commentary on the Mishnah gave rules of exegesis. There would be the citation of text, an explanation following which majors on application of the text to the situation of the interpreter, citation of opinions of the rabbis, word plays as a means of interpretation.

Those who claim the biblical writers utilized midrash are saying the human authors of scripture did creative editing in adding fictional embellishment and unhistorical fabrication in order to fulfill theological intentions. However, there could not be creation or invention of events that did not occur.[68]

Elderly pastors from the former Soviet East block have lamented,

> The churches in Eastern Europe by the end of the First War had become merely a shell without any life. The teaching of higher criticism subverted our confidence in the Scriptures and we lost our witness.[69]

David Bauer concluded source criticism, form criticism, and redaction criticism have contributed little to the advancement of our understanding of the message.[70]

Walter Kaiser explained that good exegesis cannot be built on "hypothetical sources which have never materialized in any form. These sources are deductively 'authenticated' and then inductively 'proven' from the same document in what becomes a most vicious circle."[71]

George Eldon Ladd concluded, "The historical-critical method is not an adequate method to interpret the theology of the New Testament because its presuppositions limit its findings to the exclusion of the central biblical message."[72]

John Barton in summarizing the new criticism con-

---

[68]Kantzer, "Redaction Criticism?" 1-I to 12-I; Hanna, "Biblical Inerrancy Versus Midrashic Redactionism."

[69]McAuliffe, "Everything is Broken," 15.

[70]Bauer, *The Structure of Matthew's Gospel*, 11-12.

[71]Kaiser, *Toward an Exegetical Theology*, 64.

[72]Ladd, "The Search for Perspective," 51-52.

cluded "it seems clear to me that traditional historical-critical approaches to the Bible will have to be abandoned."[73]

- Postmodernism hermeneutics

The postmodern evangelical critique of *hermeneutical criticism* . . . stands poised to speak of the normative canon and the plain sense of Scripture, resisting speculative fashion of redaction and form criticism and reader-response theories and sociopragmatic contextualizations that tyrannize and nonchalantly rape the text. . . . The classic evangelical hermeneutic trusts the apostolic primitive rememberers more than contemporary ideologically motivated advocacy deconstructionists with wild imaginations.[74]

Thomas Oden also declared

The text has rights over against its interpreters, some of whom stand poised to exploit, assault, and mug the text. When contemporary readers make themselves the absolute masters of the text, then the author has lost all rights of authorship. Authorial intent becomes subservient to contemporary ideological interests.[75]

---

[73]Barton, *Reading the Old Testament*, 184.

[74]Oden, *Requiem*, 133-134.

[75]Oden, *Requiem*, 73-74.

Jonathan Chaves concluded that postmodern hermeneutics, in its approach to language, is "profoundly anti-Christian" and that these deconstructionists are really Marxists who have applied their leftist analysis as an attack on religion and social mores.[76] In 2 Corinthians 4:2 Paul says that Christian ministers do not δολόω (*doloo*) adulterate, corrupt, or tamper with God's Word.

Robert Bork wrote in *The Tempting of America* about the battle between lawyers who hold to the "original intent" school of constitutional interpretation and the "judicial activist" school. Either the Constitution means what the framers meant to say or it means what we think it should mean. Beware of interpreters who admit they are at variance with Scripture, but assert that the Biblical writers would have agreed with them if they had been enlightened. Where the implications of Scripture collide with modern culture many will cut and paste the Scriptures rather than rebuke the culture. The most blatant reinterpretation of Scripture currently underway is the justification of homosexuality. A close second is the reinterpretation of Scripture to fit the radical feminist agenda.[77]

Statistically, the laity hold the Scripture in higher regard than their clergy. Potential pastors enter seminary to prepare for the ministry and are pumped full of critical theories about the Scriptures instead of actually giving themselves to the study of God's Word. They graduate with an exposure to all the unproven theories about the Bible and little confidence left in the Scriptures them-

---

[76]Chaves, "Soul and Reason in Literary Criticism," 828-835.

[77]See Reasoner, *Casting out Nabal and Jezebel* (2026).

selves. The danger is that conservative Bible colleges, in their desire to gain academic respectability and accreditation, import professors with impressive credentials from liberal institutions. Then these professors infect conservative denominations with the same skepticism which has killed the mainline churches and in the end the bible college is only a step behind its liberal seminary counterpart.

When our pulpits are filled by pastors who have never settled the question as to whether their faith is in the inerrant Word of God or in the latest critical theory espoused by their professors, the congregation will hear an uncertain trumpet sounded.

Can a minister entertain serious doubts concerning God's Word and at the same time possess a strong personal assurance that he or she is saved? If we have grieved the Spirit of God by doubting the Word which he inspired, how can we expect the Spirit to bear witness with our spirit? How can we test the spirits to see whether they are of God if we have no reliable touchstone?

Will a pastor-teacher who doubts the integrity of Scripture give himself to an expositional preaching ministry? Will a hungry congregation be fed the bread of life or will it be nourished on the cold stones of higher criticism?

Will God ever revive a church that does not trust and proclaim his Word? How can the church provide moral guidance for a decant society when we are playing games instead of proclaiming the Word?

In "Back to the Bible (Almost)," Roger Olson told this story.

It took quite a while for me to discern that the pastor of the church we were attending was theologically liberal. That was because he preached stirring, biblically based sermons and delivered meticulous Bible studies. I gradually began to detect, however, that he did not necessarily believe that the "truth" of the biblical stories he loved to explore and explain had any connection with objective time-and-space history. During a private conversation one Sunday morning, he revealed his true hermeneutical impulses to me: "You know," he stated, "I don't really think it matters whether any of these beautiful stories of the Bible describe what actually happened. All that really matters is their transforming power in people's lives." My family and I left that church within weeks.[78]

Is Bible Criticism Legitimate?

The work of a textual critic is to judge, to separate, to distinguish, to compare and evaluate. A critic weighs various interpretations and seeks to understand the proper meaning.

I was given a copy of *The Holman Illustrated Edition of the Holy Bible*, published in 1976. It has a misprint in 1 Timothy 6:6, "Godliness with contentment

---

[78]Olson, "Back to the Bible (Almost)," 34.

is great *pain*." Every copy of that edition I have ever seen contains the same misprint. But by doing a superficial comparison within my home I quickly determined this was *not* the correct reading. Thus, I engaged in an elementary form of textual criticism.

Literary criticism does not mean faultfinding, it means to evaluate. Biblical criticism does not have to be negative. It may mean an objective evaluation of the writing. It becomes negative when the Bible is approached with certain presuppositions. "Criticism means making intelligent judgments about historical, literary, textual, and philological questions which one must face in dealing with the Bible."[79]

> The conservatives saw themselves as *critical* scholars. They did not abandon criticism, for they, like most academics in nineteenth-century America, regarded the careful, inductive, scientific sifting of evidence as the royal road to truth. It was not criticism as such but what they perceived as prejudiced criticism, criticism corrupted by bias, unbelieving criticism, that they attacked.[80]

It is legitimate to use critical methods to establish which variant manuscript reading was the inspired original; it is illegitimate to use critical methods to call into question whether something in the original text is true. This is the distinction between lower and higher

---

[79]Ladd, *New Testament and Criticism*, 37.

[80]Noll, *Between Faith and Criticism*, 23.

criticism.

The doctrine of divine preservation holds that God has preserved what the Spirit has inspired. However, God has apparently used secondary sources, at times, to preserve his Word. There are four major sources from which the genuine reading can be determined — ancient manuscripts, ancient translations, scriptural quotations found in the works of ancient writers, and parallel passages.

At the end of the first century the Roman emperor Diocletian issued an edict to destroy all religious books. Until Constantine converted in the fourth century, early copies of the Bible were destroyed. Every copy was by hand, and these copies were also subject to natural disasters and normal conditions of decomposition.

We do not have the original autograph manuscripts. The oldest Old Testament copies we have are a thousand years after the books were originally written. While this might raise questions concerning the accuracy of the text, actually we have no cause for concern. We now possess some ten thousand Old Testament manuscripts and fragments, which includes the Masoretic Text and the Dead Sea Scrolls. The task of textual criticism is to establish the original text from the evidence.

There are five textual problems in the New Testament. The ending of Mark is the longest at 255 words. The other four combined are 306 words.[81] Out of 138,607 words in the Greek New Testament, only 561 words or 0.4% are in question. Each textual question must be resolved individually.

---

[81]The other four references are John 7:53-8:11; Acts 8:37; 1 John 5:7; Rom 8:1.

However, we have copies that go back to within one generation or less from the originals. There are 5856 handwritten New Testament Greek manuscripts, making the New Testament the best textually supported book from antiquity.

Textual critics compare the texts and determine what the original words were. Thus, we have the original text in the copies, and the original autograph can be reconstructed through a comparison process to over 99% accuracy.

A textual variant includes any variation in the wording, including word order, omission or addition of words, and even spelling differences. Variants may be neither viable nor meaningful, viable but not meaningful, meaningful but not viable, both meaningful and viable. This last category — both meaningful and viable — is by far the smallest category. One-fifth of 1% of all textual variants are significant. Not one variation affects an article of faith or a precept of duty. Even Bart Ehrman conceded, "Essential Christian beliefs are not affected by textual variants in the manuscript tradition of the New Testament."[82]

Some people accept only the Textus Receptus, asserting the superiority of this specific Greek text. The problem with claiming the Textus Receptus is the original autograph is that there are eighteen editions of the Textus Receptus and no two of them agree.[83] Although

---

[82]Ehrman, *Misquoting Jesus*, 252. Q&A section added to the 2007 paperback edition.

[83]Custer, *Truth about the King James Version Controversy*, 10.

the New King James Version of 1982 is based on this same Greek text, it is opposed by advocates of the position described in the previous paragraph. Yet the Textus Receptus normally used today was first published in 1894. There are nearly 300 differences between the KJV and the Textus Receptus. Some of the most thorough refutations of this position come from within the fundamentalist camp.[84] In his translation of the New Testament, Wesley made 12,000 changes from the KJV. About 430 of these changes indicate that he was using a Greek text other than the Textus Receptus.[85]

Those who oppose the concept of an eclectic text advocate the Majority Text approach, which determines the correct text by the number of manuscripts which agree. This is invalid because we would expect there to be fewer of the older manuscripts and more later manuscripts. The Majority text differs from the Textus Receptus in 1838 instances.

All of these disputes could be resolved if we had a complete copy of the original autographs. According to Tertullian, the original autographs of the apostles may have existed as late at the second century.[86] Perhaps

---

[84]Wisdom, "Textus Receptus: Is it Fundamental to Our Faith?"; Wood, "Question of Preservation"; MacRae and Newman, *Facts on the Textus Receptus*; Panosian, *What is the "Inspired" Word of God?*; Corner, *Critique of Gail Riplinger*.

[85]Earle, "Matthew," 81.

[86]Tertullian, "The Prescription Against Heretics," *ANF* 3:260. This evidence is evaluated by Wallace, "Did the Original New Testament Manuscripts still exist in the Second Century?"

God did not see fit to preserve the original Old and New Testament manuscripts because they would have become objects of idolatry. Ultimately, the brass serpent which God instructed Moses to make had to be destroyed by Hezekiah because it was being worshiped (2 Kgs 18:4).

God does not always disclose his purposes to us. Admittedly, God *could* have assigned an angel to superintend the preservation of the original manuscript, but errors could have still been interjected by copyists. Angels *could* have been assigned to oversee each copy that was made, but errors could have been interjected into the translation.

Again, if angels preserved the truth at every level of transmission from God to man, it would have been more efficient to assign them to preach the Word. Somehow the answer must be found in the balance between divine sovereignty and human responsibility.

When our copies agree with the original, they are just as authoritative as the original. The issue is not primarily the possession of the original autograph manuscript. Logically, it had to exist — whether or not it exists today. Through the science of textual criticism, the original *text* can be reconstructed — even if we do not possess the original document.[87]

Adam Clarke was a pioneer in the field of lower criticism or today called textual criticism — the evaluation of various manuscripts. Abel Stevens, a historian of American Methodism wrote of the influence of Adam Clarke's *Commentary*, "It may be said to have initiated

---

[87]Bahnsen, "Inerrancy of the Autographs," 160-162; Frame, *Doctrine of the Word of God*, 243.

critical biblical studies among them."[88] Where textual criticism ends, hermeneutics properly begins.

We must correctly handle the Word of truth (2 Tim 2:15). The verb ὀρθοτομέω (*orthotomeo*) means to cut a straight line. Applied to this context, the meaning is that we are commanded to guide the Word of truth along a straight line.

The authority of Scripture is nullified if its real meaning is missed. Although the Bible means what it says and generally speaks in simple terms, there are difficulties inherent in all communication. Furthermore, Christians sometimes differ regarding what Scripture teaches, therefore we need an objective standard of interpretation which avoids making the interpreter the final authority. In 1981 John Stott wrote, "It is increasingly clear to me that hermeneutics is Issue No.1 in the church today, & not least for evangelical Christians. Our differences are largely due to different ways of reading and understanding Scripture."[89]

Hermes was the Greek god who allegedly interpreted the message of the gods to humans. The verb ἑρμηνεύω (*hermeneuo*) is used in Luke 24:27 where Christ interprets or explains the Old Testament. It means to verbalize, translate, and explain. This word, in various forms, is used in Matthew 1:23; Mark 5:41, 15:22,34; John 1:8,38, 9:7; Acts 4:36, 9:36, 13:8; 1 Corinthians 12: 10, 14:28; Hebrews 7:2.

The task of hermeneutics is to ascertain what God has said in Scripture; to determine the meaning of the

---

[88]Stevens, *Life and Times of Nathan Bangs,* 190.

[89]Chapman, *Godly Ambition,* 105.

Word of God. Walter Kaiser wrote, "The primary task of the biblical scholar is to unfold the meaning of the text of Scripture as it was originally intended to be understood by the writer of that text."[90] Packer stated, "Biblical authority is an empty notion unless we know how to determine what the Bible means."[91]

---

[90]Kaiser, "Literary Form of Genesis 1-11," 48.

[91]Packer, "Hermeneutics and Biblical Authority," 3.

William Burt Pope wrote, "The first law should be fidelity to Holy Scripture, which is the supreme standard in the Church both of the worship offered by the people to God and of God's instruction of His people." Above all, preaching should be a faithful interpretation of the Word which is based upon its literal grammatical meaning and its intention as found in the whole of Scripture. This implied the necessity of studying the text in its original language, or by the help of commentators, and according to the laws of interpretation.

These laws pertain to the methods of interpreting figurative language, that which is common and that which is peculiar to language itself, the observance of the context of every passage and its connection with the writer's general system of teaching, recognition of the analogy of faith, and the absolute necessity of a spiritual sympathy with the sacred word under the direct influence of the Holy Spirit.[92]

Even though all Scripture is profitable, all Scripture is not profitable for the same purposes.

- The law of non-contradiction

A true contradiction is to both affirm and deny the same reality. For the Bible to assert genuine contradictions would mean that it could not have been inspired by the source of all truth. If Scripture contains legitimate

---

[92]Moss, *W. B. Pope*, 79, 94-96.

contradictions, we have no way of knowing which time God was right and therefore we must rely on an "expert" — who then replaces Scripture as our final authority.

The Bible assumes the validity of the law of non-contradiction when it states

- No man can serve two masters (Matt 6:24).
- A good tree cannot produce bad fruit (Matt 7:18).
- He who is not with me is against me (Matt 12:30).

"To tolerate contradiction is to be indifferent to truth."[93] Terry wrote, "It is not to be supposed that any fact of nature or history can be in conflict with the express declarations of the omniscient God. . . . Truth of whatever kind can never be in real conflict with each other."[94] Clark Pinnock wrote, "Scripture honors the law of non-contradiction, and operates on the basis of a correspondence idea of truth."[95] Bernard Ramm explained that belief in the inerrancy of the Scriptures leads us to affirm there are no contradictions in the Bible.[96]

However, Ramm eventually became enamored with Barth, who denied the law of non-contradiction.[97] Barth adopted the modern Hegelian method of dialectics,[98]

---

[93]Flew, *Thinking Straight*, 15.

[94]Terry, *Biblical Hermeneutics*, 583.

[95]Pinnock, *Biblical Revelation*, 192.

[96]Ramm, *Protestant Biblical Interpretation*, 205.

[97]Barth, *Church Dogmatics* 1/1, 8.

[98]Kelly, *Systematic Theology*, 2:289.

often presented as paradox. However, a *paradox* is actually an *apparent* contradiction. *Paradox* is a valid term; the dialectic method is not a valid method. This amounts to making the reader think he has affirmed truth, then moving on to deny it. Under the influence of Barth, Ramm claimed that the traditional view of inspiration "*materializes* the Holy Scripture, and in so materializing it robbed Scripture of its *spiritual* and *dynamic* quality." Ramm explained that *materialization* means that the Word of God is reduced literally to a book that one can carry around in one's pocket. "The Word of God in its spiritual dimension has been lost."[99]

But if there is always a distance between the Word of God and what the human authors wrote, due to language and culture, and if there is also a distance because of the sinfulness of the human authors, Barth said that we must *seek* the Word of God in the text. However, if we are also sinful and are also bound by the restraints of language, how can we ever know truth?

Barth worried that if we found errors in Scripture, then God would be the cause of our unbelief. Therefore, he declared that if God is not ashamed of errors in the Scripture, why should we be?[100] The task of biblical scholarship, however, should not be to hunt for mistakes but to attempt reconciliation of apparent discrepancies.

While the Bible is trustworthy and accurate, it should not be expected to comport with modern technical precision in matters of chronology. Variations in reporting an event do not necessarily constitute a contradic-

---

[99]Ramm, *After Fundamentalism*, 122; 118.

[100]Barth, *Church Dogmatics*, I/2, 531.

tion.

Many apparent contradictions are resolved when we
see them in the light of the whole of Scripture. However,
the Bible does contain paradoxes. Augustine explained,

> If we are perplexed by an apparent contradic-
> tion in Scripture, it is not allowable to say, The
> author of this book is mistaken; but either the
> manuscript is faulty, or the translation is wrong,
> or you have not understood.[101]

The task of systematic theology is not to pick portions of Scripture which support a preconceived doctrinal
position, but rather to reconcile apparent contradictory
statements in Scripture.

Martin Luther struggled to reconcile the theology of
Paul against that of James regarding salvation by faith
and works. Luther's reaction to the doctrine of salvation
by works in James was to declare that it was really an
epistle of straw which did not contain the gospel and
casting doubt on the apostleship of James.[102]

Marcion may have been the first to depreciate the
Old Testament, but not the last. Dispensationalism tends
to pit law against grace; the Old Testament against the
New Testament.[103]

---

[101]Augustine, "Reply to Faustus the Manichean," 4.11.5; *NPNF*1
4:180.

[102]Rittgers, *RCS*, 13:200-201.

[103]Allis, "Modern Dispensationalism," 24. Ironically, C. I.
Scofield wrote *Rightly Dividing the Word of Truth* (1936),
which is the classic illustration of how to do it wrong!

For example, Proverbs 24:13 says to eat honey; 25:27 it is not good to eat too much honey. Is this a contradiction? It would be a very juvenile author who would contradict himself this blatantly. I make the assumption that Solomon is using this technique to get our attention

Are we looking for contradictions? If so we will find apparent contradictions. However, if we approach the scripture believing it to be rational, we can understand its meaning — sometimes with the help of a good commentary. The meaning of Proverbs 25:4-5 is that one should not lower himself to the level of a fool but that there are times when the lesser evil is to speak out than be silent. Ignore foolish statements when you can, but address them when you must.

- Clarity

The perspicuity of Scripture refers to its inherent clarity. The Reformer John Knox explained,

> The Word of God is plain in itself. If there appear any obscurity in one place, the Holy Ghost, which is never contrarious to Himself, explaineth the same more clearly in other places; so that there can remain no doubt, but unto such as obstinately will remain ignorant.[104]

Martin Luther responded to the claims by Erasmus that the Scripture was obscure, "If Scripture is obscure or equivocal, why need it have been brought down to us

---

[104]Knox, *History of the Reformation in Scotland*, 280.

by act of God?" Luther wrote,

> I certainly grant that many *passages* in the
> Scriptures are obscure and hard to elucidate,
> but that is due, not to the exalted nature of their
> subject, but to our own linguistic and grammati-
> cal ignorance; and it does not in any way pre-
> vent us knowing all the *contents* of Scripture.

Luther contended that if anyone finds the Bible
wholly obscure, the fault is not in the Bible, but in him —
he is spiritually blind, cannot discern Christ, and needs
the help of the Holy Spirit to make him see.[105]
Wesley agreed with Luther that theology is nothing
but a grammar of the language of the Holy Ghost.[106] The
Bible makes sense and can be understood through the
application of our mind and the illumination of the Holy
Spirit. Wesley explained, "We need the same Spirit to
understand the Scripture which enabled the holy men of
old to *write* it."[107] The Word of God is spiritual and
therefore can only be spiritually perceived (1 Cor 2:14).
Yet the Holy Spirit does not bypass our mind. This does
not imply that a non-Christian is unable to understand
the meaning of any Scripture. It means that without the
regeneration of the Holy Spirit, the sinner will not wel-
come the message. Understanding is more of an issue of

---

[105]Luther, *Bondage of the Will*, 128; 70-74.

[106]Wesley, *Notes*, 6. Wesley used the word *divinity* instead of
theology.

[107]Wesley, *Letter* to the Lord Bishop of Gloucester, 2.10. *BE
Works*, 11:509.

the will than of the intellect.

While every passage is not equally clear, Frame concluded "Scripture is always clear enough for us to carry out our present responsibilities before God."[108]

How to delineate how much or what part of Biblical Exegesis is attributable to mere human efforts and how much or what part comes from the Holy Spirit is difficult, if not impossible. Even an unenlightened unbeliever can glean some of the meaning if he follows correct procedure, but somewhere his efforts will go awry because he lacks spiritual insight. On the other hand, the enlightened believer will not, in most cases, be conscious of what has come from the Spirit as distinguished from what comes from the science of Exegesis. It will be the combined effect of the two that will bring him to the correct interpretation. Of course, he also needs the Spirit's guidance to apply the interpretation to life as it is now, but this is quite distinct from His help in illuminating the meaning of the passage in reference to its original setting.[109]

Instead of the inadequate position of soteriological inerrancy, a more adequate position is soteriological perspicuity. All Scripture is God-breathed and therefore true, but not all Scripture is equally clear. However, the way of salvation is so clear that even a fool need not go

---

[108]Frame, *Doctrine of the Word of God*, 207.

[109]Thomas, *Introduction to Exegesis*, 15-16.

astray (Isa 35:8).

- The Analogy of Faith

Where the Bible is not clear, obscure passages are interpreted in light of clearer passages. Terry explained,

> No single statement or obscure passage of one book can be allowed to set aside a doctrine which is clearly established by many passages. The obscure texts must be interpreted in the light of those which are plain and positive. . . . No doctrine which rests upon a single passage of Scripture can belong to fundamental doctrines recognized in the analogy of faith.[110]

There is an analogy of faith or an internal consistency and harmony within Scripture. William Cooke declared, "If the Bible is in harmony with truth, it will harmonize with itself."[111] John Wesley commented on the *oracles of God*:

> That grand scheme of doctrine which is delivered therein, touching original sin, justification by faith, and present, inward salvation. There is a wonderful analogy between all these; and a close and intimate connection between the chief heads of that faith "which was once delivered to the saints." Every article, therefore, concerning

---

[110]Terry, *Biblical Hermeneutics*, 579; 581.

[111]Cooke, *Christian Theology*, 24.

which there is any question should be determined by this rule; every doubtful scripture interpreted according to the grand truths which run through the whole.[112]

The term *analogy of faith* is found only in Romans 12:6. There it means the proportion of faith given to each believer.[113] Theologically, *the analogy of faith* describes the method of interpreting the parts of Scripture, especially difficult and obscure ones, consistent with the whole of Scripture. Thus, the *analogy of faith* in Romans 12:6 was interpreted by Wesley as a reference to the body of Christian doctrine.[114]

• Genres

It is helpful to be aware of literature types, yet the Bible is one book and we should not build walls between sections of the Bible.

If we try to use the rules for interpreting one genre to interpret a different type, we will almost surely misinterpret the passage that we are studying. We cannot, for example, read a psalm in the same way that we read a parable. This should not be surprising. We know from our own culture that we cannot read a phone book as if it were a novel, a shopping list as if it were

---

[112]Wesley, *Notes*, 397.

[113]Ramm, *Protestant Biblical Interpretation*, 107.

[114]Wesley, *Notes*, 397.

an advertisement, a poem as if it were a court brief.[115]

Depending on how the categories are determined, there are approximately ten basic genres found in Scripture — law, Old Testament narrative, psalms, wisdom literature, prophecy, gospel, parables, New Testament history, epistle, and apocalyptic literature. Each type of literature may have specific parameters which need to be taken into account.

Identifying Literary Genres

- Reading the law

Basic law is a declaration of principle. Case law in the application of the basic law within Jewish culture. The New Testament provides a broader interpretation of the law.

For example, the basic law declares "You shall not steal" (Exod 20:15). In Jewish culture this meant, among other things, "Do not muzzle an ox while it is treading out the grain (Deut 25:4). This principle is applied in 1 Corinthians 9:3-14; 1 Timothy 5:17:18 to teach that a minister has a right to a salary.[116]

Basic law is a reflection of the nature of God and cannot be abolished. Wesley taught that the moral law is eternal. It is a copy of the eternal mind, a transcript of

---

[115]Stuart, "Interpret = Understand + Explain," 12.

[116]Rushdoony, *Institutes of Biblical Law*, 11-12.

the divine nature.[117] Although every believer is free from the Jewish ceremonial law, the entire Mosaic dispensation, and even the moral law as a means of procuring justification, we are not through with the law.[118] The moral law cannot pass away since it is a reflection of God's nature. In 1 Corinthians 9:20-21 Paul says he is not under the law, yet in the next verse he clarifies that statement to mean that he is not free from God's law. He is still under the law of Christ. According to Romans 8:2 we are under a new law — the law of the Spirit of life. Wesley argued that Christ did not free us from his own law.[119] According to James 1:25, those who continue to live by the perfect law, motivated by love, are free. Those who do not live by the law of God are slaves to sin and criminals before God.[120]

Case law reflects how "constitutional law" was applied. These applications are not necessarily valid today. Ceremonial law was fulfilled in Christ and is no longer binding, yet the principles they taught are still valid.[121]

The failure to make this distinction leads either to lawlessness or legalism. This distinction between the ceremonial law and the moral law is implied in such passages as Psalm 40:6-8, 51:16-17; Isaiah 1:11-17; Hosea 6:6; and Micah 6:6-8. Jesus taught in Matthew 12:11-12

---

[117]Wesley, "Original, Nature, Properties, and Use of the Law," Sermon #34, 2.1-6.

[118]Wesley, "Sermon on the Mount, V," Sermon #25, 1.1.

[119]Wesley, *BE Works*, 14:52-54.

[120]Wesley, *Notes*, 599.

[121]Bahnsen, *By This Standard*, 135-138.

that some ritual laws could be preempted by acts of mercy. In Matthew 23:23 Jesus taught that justice, mercy, and faithfulness carried more weight than the ritual duty of tithing herbs, which were not specifically covered in Leviticus 27:30 and Deuteronomy 14:22. Paul also distinguished between the importance of dietary law and sexual morality (1 Cor 6:13).

However, the category of moral law is rejected by dispensationalists because they relegate it to the Mosaic dispensation. Showers argued that, in contrast with covenant theology, dispensationalism holds the position that "Christians today are not under any aspect of the Mosaic Law, even the moral aspect."[122]

- Reading Old Testament Narrative

The historical record of Scripture tells us what *did* happen, not necessarily what we should do. Michael Heiser makes the claim that while all Scripture is inspired, not all Scripture contains truth claims. He then rejects "literalism," which for him means that if the Bible record it — the Bible endorses it. He then deals with polygamy and slavery which are recorded but not commanded.[123]

A basic fallacy is to claim the first eleven chapters of Genesis are poetic and are not to be taken literally. Yet suddenly the same document becomes historical at chapter 12. Genesis covers creation, the fall, the flood, and the tower in the first eleven chapters. Chapters 12-50 cover

---

[122]Showers, *There Really Is a Difference*, 187.

[123]Heiser, "Inspiration of Scripture Explained."

Abraham, Isaac, Jacob, and Joseph. It is all history.

The Bible does contain poetic accounts of creation in Job 38:4-11; Psalm 8, 19:1-6, 102:25,104. These accounts should be compared to the Genesis account. The figurative use of language as found in the poetic literature is not present in Genesis. Nor does the narrative have any of the characteristics of a parable.[124] Walter Kaiser wrote,

> There are 64 geographical terms, 88 personal names, 48 generic names and at least 21 identifiable cultural items (such as gold, bdellium, onyx, brass, iron, gopher wood, bitumen, mortar, brick, stone, harp, pipe, cities, towers) in those opening chapters. The significance of this list may be seen by comparing it, for example, with "the paucity of references in the Koran. The single tenth chapter of Genesis has five times more geographical data of importance than the whole of the Koran." Every one of these items presents us with the possibility of establishing the reliability of our author. The content runs head on into a description of the real world rather than recounting events belonging to another world or level of reality.[125]

Fee and Stuart warned that Old Testament narratives are not allegories or stories filled with hidden

---

[124]Young, *In the Beginning*, 13,18-19; Currid, "Cosmology of History," 44-45.

[125]Kaiser, "Literary Form of Genesis 1-11," 59.

meaning. Individual Old Testament narratives are not intended to teach moral lessons, however, they often illustrate what is taught explicitly elsewhere.[126]

- Reading New Testament History

Acts is the historical book of the New Testament. It is a record what happened, not necessarily what should happen. The Holy Spirit was poured out six times. Each occurrence was different. However, Pentecostals claim that everyone must speak in tongues as the initial evidence that they have been baptized with the Holy Spirit. However, in three instances where the Spirit was given, tongues-speaking did *not* occur. The variation in the historical record may have been Luke's purpose in order to show what was *not* essential. All believers have the Holy Spirit (Rom 8:9), and there is no command in the New Testament for Christians to receive the baptism with the Holy Spirit. Any person who does not have the Spirit of Christ dwelling in him and governing him is "not a Christian; not in a state of salvation," according to Wesley.[127]

John Stott explained that the

> revelation of the purpose of God in Scripture should be sought primarily in its *didactic* rather than its *descriptive* parts. More precisely, we should look for it in the teaching of Jesus and in

---

[126]Fee and Stuart, *How to Read the Bible for All Its Worth*, 92.

[127]Wesley, *Notes*, 381.

the sermons and writings of the apostles, rather than in the purely narrative portions of Acts. . . . I am *not* saying that the descriptive passages of the Bible are valueless, for "all Scripture is inspired by God and profitable" (2 Tim 3:16). What I *am* saying is that what is descriptive is valuable only in so far as it is interpreted by what is didactic.[128]

Gordon Fee, who is a Pentecostal theologian, wrote, "Our assumption, along with many others, is this: *Unless Scripture explicitly tells us we must do something, what is only narrated or described can never function in a normative way.*"[129]

Furthermore, the early church sold everything and shared their resources. However, this attempt failed. In Acts 11:30 relief was raised for the brethren living in Judea. There was a great famine in the whole world in the days of Claudius Caesar. This voluntary plan, which seemed so successful at first, had utterly failed within fifteen years.

In Romans 15:26 Paul again collected an offering from the gentile churches for the poor saints in Jerusalem around AD 52-57. Why were they poor? They did not have any assets and were relying on the benevolence of others. Such benevolence cannot be sustained long-term. The general principle is personal responsibility. "If a man will not work, he shall not eat" (2 Thess 3:10).

---

[128]Stott, *Baptism and Fullness*, 15..

[129]Fee and Stuart, *How to Read the Bible for All Its Worth*, 118-119.

Furthermore, this early form of communism was not commanded—merely reported. I think history can verify that every communal society failed. Socialism has never worked because it destroys the incentive to work.

W. B. Pole concluded that the voluntary communism in Acts 2:44 was extraordinary, temporary, and binding on no one. He affirmed the right to private property and capitalism.[130]

- Reading Poetry

Hebrew poetry did not rhyme, but it was parallel. This humorous example makes the point:

> I hit him on the head,
> I smote him on the pate,
> Yea, upon his noggin I did knock him.

So how many times was this unfortunate man assaulted? If this is prose, he got whacked three times. If this is poetic, he got whacked once.

-
- Reading Wisdom Literature

Wisdom literature utilizes aphorisms or pithy sayings. The *sitz en laben*, or life situation, is a parent

---

[130]Pope, *Compendium*, 3:249-253; see also Summers, *Systematic Theology*, 2:507-510. Gregg observed that private property was still owned by Christians in Acts 9:11, 10:32, 12:12, 16:40, 17:5, 18:7, 21:8; Rom 16:5; Phlm 2 [*Empire of the Risen Son*, 249].

teaching a child. A proverb is a generalization. Unlike most of Scripure, Proverbs 10-31 has no context from one verse to the next; the broader context is wisdom statements.

• Reading Gospels

The four Gospels are technically not biographies in the modern sense. They are historically accurate but the four evangelists choose from that historical records what is needed to make their point. John closes his Gospel with the hyperbolic statement that the cosmos was not enough a big enough library to contain exhaustive revelation (John 20-30-31). What John did select was *not* fabricated, however.

• Reading parables

A parable is an extended metaphor or simile which compares spiritual truth with common experience. It is frequently defined as an earthy story with a heavenly meaning. Literally, the word means to place two things alongside each other for comparison. A parable is intended to illustrate one main point. Another common statement about parables warns that "they were not meant to walk on all four feet."
"In preaching parables and similitudes, great care should be taken to discover their *object* and *design*, and those grand and leading circumstances by which the author illustrates his subjects."[131]

---

[131]Clarke, *Commentary*, 5:155.

The parable of the ten virgins illustrates the need for readiness. However, it has been misused

- by Arminian to prove it is possible to fall from grace.
- by Calvinists to prove there may be professions of faith which are not genuine
- by American holiness advocates to prove a second blessing is necessary in order to get to heaven
- by dispensationalists to prove a partial rapture

A parable cannot be used to *prove* any doctrine. Doctrine must be established from those passages which are teaching doctrine. A parable then can be utilized to *illustrate* doctrine.

- Reading epistles

Scripture contains twenty-one letters written to specific congregations or individuals in the first century. No valid interpretation of these instructions can contain anything which would not make sense to the primary audience to whom it was written. Thus, we must first identify what issue the author was addressing then and how that teaching applies to us now. Fee and Stuart explain that "a text cannot mean what it never could have meant to its author or his or her readers. . . . Whenever we share comparable particulars with first-century hearers, God's Word to us is the same as his Word to them."[132]

---

[132]Fee and Stuart, *How to Read the Bible for All Its Worth*, 74-75.

- Reading prophecy

The father of dispensationalism, John Darby, advocated a strict literalism in the interpretation of Scripture, especially its prophetic parts.[133]Dispensationalism tends to literalize what is symbolic and allegorize what is historical.

However, prophetic and apocalyptic literature frequently employ symbolism. Taking the Bible literally means interpreting the Bible according to the rules of grammar and the facts of history. It does not imply the disregard for symbolism, especially when it is apparent that the context is symbolic. Symbolism and images, however, are not a code, they do not exist in isolation, and we need biblical indication for any symbol, type, or image.[134]

The prophets utilized symbols and figures which they borrowed from history, culture, and creation. Their message was often received in a vision or a dream. Fee and Stuart remind us that while the prophets did indeed predict future events, for the most part those events are now past.[135]

Fulfilled prophecy is the key for interpreting unfulfilled prophecy. Crenshaw and Gunn analyzed 97 Old Testament prophecies cited in the book of Matthew.

---

[133]Bass, *Backgrounds to Dispensationalism*, 21-24.

[134]Jordan, *Through New Eyes*, 15-16.

[135]Fee and Stuart, *How to Read the Bible for All Its Worth*, 199-200.

Only 34, or 35%, were literally fulfilled.[136]

- Reading apocalyptic literature

Daniel and Revelation are considered to be apocalyptic literature by some scholars. Other scholars deny there is such a category. This debate hinges on the definition of *apocalyptic*. They are at least prophetic. Those who make a distinction explain that the prophets typically rebuked Israel for going astray. The message was usually given in the form of an analogy. It was poetic and corrective.

In apocalyptic literature the message is written as an encouragement for the faithful. No one interprets the book of Revelation in a consistently literal way. Commenting on Revelation 20, Beale explained,

> Because the objects he sees and what he hears are seen and heard in a vision, they are not *first* to be understood literally but viewed as symbolically portrayed and communicated, which is the *symbolic* level of the vision. That this vision is shot through with symbols is apparent merely from the obviously symbolic nature of such words as "chain," "abyss," "dragon," "serpent," "locked," "sealed," and "beast."[137]

---

[136]Crenshaw and Gunn, *Dispensationalism Today, Yesterday, and Tomorrow*, 22.

[137]Beale, *Revelation*, 974. See also Tenney, *Interpreting Revelation*, 186-193.

In reaction to those who fail to grasp the poetic style of the book of Revelation, Chesterton said, "Though St. John the Evangelist saw many strange monsters in his vision, he saw no creature so wild as one of his own commentators."[138]

Bible symbolism and imagery is not a code. These symbols do not exist in isolation. We must always have a clear-cut biblical indication for any symbol or image we think we have found.[139] A working knowledge of Scripture is prerequisite for understand apocalyptic literature. The book of Revelation contains 348 quotes or allusions to the Old Testament. There is a reason it is the final book. It requires a grasp of the first sixty-five books!

Three Keys to the Book of Revelation

1. Jesus Christ is the central character. The first Greek word is ἀποκάλυσις (*apokalupsis*), meaning unveiling or revelation. The subject is not everything you ever wanted to know about the future. This book is the revelation of Jesus Christ. According to 19:10, "the testimony of Jesus is the spirit of prophecy."

2. The first century is the time frame. Kenneth Gentry wrote, "The closer we get to the year 2000, the farther we get from the events of Revelation."[140]

The first verse of this book also establishes that it

---

[138]Chesterton, *Orthodoxy*, 29.

[139]Jordan, *Through New Eyes*, 15-17.

[140]Gentry, "A Preterist View of Revelation," 37.

deals with things which "must soon take place." Twelve more times throughout the book either the unfolding of the book or the coming of Christ is said to be *soon*. Bruce Metzger wrote, "The word *soon* indicates that John intended his message for his own generation."[141]

However, ever reference to the coming of Christ does not necessary describe his second advent.

- Christ came to the disciples after his resurrection.
- Christ came on the day of Pentecost.
- Christ came in judgment on Jerusalem in AD 70.[142]
- Christ comes for the Christian at death.
- Christ comes often in judgment (Rev 2:5,16).
- Christ comes often in revival.
- Christ comes to the believer in salvation.

A radical preterist position holds that every eschatological event occurred in the first century. This is heretical.[143] However, a moderate preterist interpretation makes the book meaningful for those who first received it and gives room for a universal application of the message of the book.[144] A moderate preterist position acknowledges that there are future events, such as the return of Christ. R. C. Sproul concluded, "I am convinced that only within the framework of a moderate preterist

---

[141]Metzger, *Breaking the Code*, 21.

[142]Steele, *Half-Hours with St. John's Epistles*, xii.

[143]See Gregg, *Why Not Full-Preterism?* (2022); Gentry, *Have We Missed the Second Coming?* (2016).

[144]Summers, *Worthy is the Lamb*, 44-45.

position can we escape the devastating assault of the critics."[145]

Yet John MacArthur made the incredible claim that "anything other than the futurist approach leaves the meaning of the book to human ingenuity and opinion."[146] No approach, however, has been more subjective and open to manipulation than the futurist attempt to read current events into the text.

3. The style of writing is specified as symbolic. The Greek verb σημαίνω (*semaino*) means to give a sign or to express by signs or symbols. Tenny explained that this word means figurative, symbolic, or imaginative communication, and is intended to convey the truth by picture rather than by definition.[147]

- Priority of the original language

The original Hebrew and Greek text is the final authority in matters of translation. Every translation should start with the original text.

A strict holiness woman once declared that it was wrong for a woman to curl her hair. When I told her that was not borne out in the Greek New Testament she countered that it was in the Spanish New Testament. I was never able to establish with her the priority of the original language. She seemed to feel that her Spanish translation was just as authoritative as my Greek

---

[145]Sproul, "A Journey Back in Time," 7.

[146]MacArthur, *Revelation 1-11*, 9-11.

[147]Tenny, *Interpreting Revelation*, 186.

Testament!

- One basic meaning; many applications

During the mediaeval period the prevalent approach to Bible interpretation held that the text had four levels of meaning. The lowest level was the historical or literal meaning. Then the spiritual or typological meaning followed. Next was the tropological or moral meaning, followed by the anagogical or future meaning. Of course, this approach had the effect of discouraging the non-professional from even reading, much less understanding the Bible.

What a passage means is fixed by the author and discovered by the reader. Wesley explained,

> I apply no Scripture phrase either to myself or any other without carefully considering, bot the *original* meaning and the *secondary* sense, wherein (allowing for different times and circumstances) it may be applied to ordinary Christians.[148]

Scripture has one basic meaning, but is capable of many applications.[149] This principle was articulated in 1643 by William Ames,

> There is only one meaning for every place in Scripture. Otherwise the meaning of Scripture

---

[148]Wesley, *BE Works*, 9:116.

[149]Terry, *Biblical Hermeneutics*, 511-513.

would not only be unclear and uncertain, but there would be no meaning at all — for anything which does not mean one thing surely means nothing.[150]

Regarding prophetic passages, Milton S. Terry was emphatic that there is no double sense.

> A fundamental principle in grammatico-historical exposition is that words and sentences can have but one signification in one and the same connection. The moment we neglect this principle we drift out upon a sea of uncertainty and conjecture.[151]

Terry quoted John Owen, "If the Scripture has more than one meaning, it has no meaning at all." Scripture has one specific meaning, and the object of the interpreter is to determine what the passage means and adhere rigidly to that meaning.[152] This single sense amounts to the author's intended meaning. The primary task of the interpreter is to recognize the meaning which the author intended and to exegete the implications of that meaning.

Bloesch concluded, "While the text has a single, objective meaning that corresponds to the intention of the original author, its significance will vary as it is ap-

---

[150]Ames, *The Marrow of Theology*, 188.

[151]Terry, *Biblical Hermeneutics*, 205.

[152]Terry, *Biblical Hermeneutics*, 493-499. For a more recent discussion, see Bloesch, *Holy Scripture*, 184-192.

plied to different situations."[153]

However, this principle does not negate the existence of typology in Scripture. A *type* is a person, institution, office, event, or action in the Old Testament which has symbolic significance regarding something future in the New Testament.

Yet some Old Testament passages do not always seem to be used in the New Testament with reference to their original context. Frame believes that in such cases the New Testament is making an application of the Old Testament text.[154] The same Holy Spirit who inspired the original truth has the prerogative to assign a different meaning to the same words. We do not have that prerogative.[155]

Some theologians, however, believe that along with the literal sense, the Holy Spirit may encode a hidden meaning. This fuller sense is implied in the Latin phrase *sensus plenior*. While the author himself may not grasp the full implication of his message, *fuller sense* does not imply a different meaning. Daniel did not understand all of his vision (12:8-9). In fact, Packer stated with regard to all Scripture, "God's meaning and message through each passage, when set in its total biblical context, exceeds what the human writer had in mind."[156]

---

[153]Bloesch, *Holy Scripture*, 189.

[154]Frame, *Doctrine of the Word of God*, 190-193.

[155]Bahnsen, "Inerrancy of the Autographa," 170-171;. See also Beale and Carson, *Commentary on the New Testament Use of the Old Testament*.

[156]Packer, "Biblical Authority, Hermeneutics and Inerrancy," 147.

Without limiting the illumination of the Holy Spirit, the text has one basic meaning but multiple applications. Regarding application Wesley wrote,

> I apply no Scripture phrase either to myself or any other without carefully considering, both the original meaning and the secondary sense, wherein (allowing for different times and circumstances) it may be applied to ordinary Christians.[157]

- The centrality of Christ

Jesus Christ is the climax of God's special revelation. He is the unveiled mystery of God (Col 1:27, 2:2, 4:3). He is the divine wisdom. His coming marked the beginning of the last days. As the *logos* of God, he is the mediating agent in creation, in redemption, and in coming judgment.

Augustine is famous for stating that Christ is concealed in the Old Testament and revealed in the New Testament.[158] Pope defined revelation as the unfolding of the eternal counsel of God in Christ. He is the personal revelation of God. The sum and substance of truth is found in him (Eph 4:21). "His testimony is the last word of all objective revelation."[159]

Jesus began with Moses and all the prophets, ex-

---

[157]Wesley, *Letter* to John Church, 2 Feb 1745, 3.5.

[158]Augustine, *Expositions on Psalms*, Psalm 106, ¶ 32; *NP-NF*1 8:531.

[159]Pope, *Compendium*, 1:38.

plaining everything they said concerning him (Luke 24:27,44).[160] Jesus declared that the Scriptures testify concerning him (John 5:39,46). Martin Luther referred to Christ as the "star and kernel" of Scripture, "the center part of the circle" about which everything else revolves.[161] He is the key to knowledge (Luke 11:52). Yet the authority of Scripture cannot be reduced solely to its function of directing us to Christ.

Pope taught the "hydrostatic law" of exegesis, meaning that the water in the Epistles never rises above its source in the Gospels. Thus, our union with God in Christ through the Holy Spirit is the basis of the Christian's perfection.[162]

• Context

A familiar quip is that text without a context is a pretext! The best commentary on Scripture is Scripture. An obscure verse must be interpreted in its broader setting. The Bible contains quotations from pagan philosophers (Acts 17:28), from demons (Mark 5:9), from Satan (Job 1:9), as well as Job's misguided counselors. We must distinguish between what Scripture reports and what it teaches. Scripture records without error statements which are false. It is incumbent upon the interpreter to pay attention to the context.

• Cross reference

---

[160]see Hodgkin, *Christ in All the Scriptures.*

[161]Olsen, "The Christ Alone," 6.

[162]Moss, *W. B. Pope*, 105.

Use Scripture to interpret Scripture. Compare parallel passages. Look at the use of the same word in other passages. This technique used to be called *uses loquendi*, which describes the meaning of the term in current usage as employed by a particular writer or prevalent in a particular period of time.

• Historical and cultural background

We must avoid two opposing errors. On the one hand we live in a world of technical expertise. We may create the perception that reading the Bible is a daunting challenge best left to the experts if we over-emphasize the fact that we have cultural blinders and cannot understand the ancient world of the Bible. While the Roman Catholic church claims that only the institution can determine what the text means, in Protestant circles, too often, we are told that only the experts can determine what the text means.

Yet Scripture transcends cultural barriers. If it takes an expert to tell you what God said, then he did not communicate very clearly! Tyndale declared that if God spared his life, ere many years he would cause a boy that drove the plough to know more of the Scripture than the Pope.[163]

The 1982 Chicago Statement on Hermeneutics, formulated by the International Council on Biblical Inerrancy, stated:

------

[163]Foxe, *Foxe's Book of Martyrs*, ch 12.

WE AFFIRM that translations of the text of Scripture can communicate knowledge of God across all temporal and cultural boundaries. WE DENY that the meaning of biblical texts is so tied to the culture out of which they came that understanding of the same meaning in other cultures is impossible.[164]

On the other hand, we need to understand the languages and grammar, as well as the historical background in order to avoid common mistakes. Extra-biblical data does have value in clarifying what Scripture teaches and for prompting correction of faulty interpretations. However, extra-biblical views cannot be used to disprove Scripture or hold priority over it.

Dealing with Difficult Passages

Some biblical passages are difficult to understand. Others may be difficult to accept. Here we are dealing with statements that are difficult to reconcile.

The careful reader will occasionally discover statements in Scripture which appear to be contradictions. According to Terry, such problems are found in the genealogical tables and in various numerical, historical, doctrinal, ethical, and prophetic statements.

The interpreter should not ignore the difficulty, but should attempt to explain the apparent inconsistency by rational methods.

---

[164]Radmacher and Preus, *Hermeneutics, Inerrancy, and the Bible*, 884.

It does not follow that because he is not able to solve the problem it is therefore insoluble. The lack of sufficient data has often effectually baffled the efforts of the most able and accomplished exegetes.

Terry explained that most discrepancies are the errors of copyists, the variety of names applied to the same person or place, different methods of reckoning times and seasons, different local and historical standpoints, and the special scope and plan of each particular book. "Variations are not contradictions, and many essential variations arise from different methods of arranging a series of particular facts."[165]

Those who are looking for contradictions tend to find what they are looking for. However, if we approach the Scripture believing it to be rational, we can understand its meaning — sometimes with the help of a good commentary. Concerning Bible difficulties, Gleason Archer counseled,

Be fully persuaded in your own mind that an adequate explanation exists, even though you have not yet found it. . . . Avoid the fallacy of shifting from one a priori to its opposite every time an apparent problem arises. The Bible is either the inerrant Word of God or else it is an imperfect record by fallible men. Once we have come into agreement with Jesus that the Scripture is completely trustworthy and authoritative, then it is out of the question for us to shift

---

[165]Terry, *Biblical Hermeneutics*, 514.

over to the opposite assumption, that the Bible is only the errant record of fallible men as they wrote about God. If the Bible is truly the Word of God, as Jesus said, then it must be treated with respect, trust, and complete obedience.... Carefully study the context and framework of the verse in which the problem arises until you gain some idea of what the verse is intended to mean within its own setting. . . . No interpretation of Scripture is valid that is not based on careful exegesis. . . . In the case of parallel passages, the only method that can be justified is harmonization. . . .Whenever historical accounts of the Bible are called into question on the basis of alleged disagreement with the finds of archaeology or the testimony of ancient non-Hebrew documents, always remember that the Bible is itself an archaeological document of the highest caliber. It is simply crass bias for critics to hold that whenever a pagan record disagrees with the biblical account, it must be the Hebrew author that was in error.[166]

Nelson Glueck declared, "No archaeological discovery has ever controverted a single properly understood Biblical statement."[167]

The Bible speaks in ordinary language. We should not expect technical precision, exhaustive detail, or complete comprehensiveness. We must distinguish be-

---

[166]Archer, *Encyclopedia of Bible Difficulties*, 15-17.

[167]Glueck, *Rivers in the Desert*, 136.

tween imprecision and error. Biblical history is truthful but incomplete. It does not comport with modern ideals of historiography. Yet incompleteness does not negate infallibility.

The language employed in Scripture is that of simple observation, not scientific empiricism. Thus, phenomenal language, as well as figurative and symbolic language, does not imply a woeful ignorance in ancient civilizations.

> Virtually all of the criticisms of cosmographic references in the Bible can be shown to be distortions of the texts, for a proper hermeneutic recognizes the frequent use of phenomenological language and of poetic imagery, including figures of speech like metaphors, similes, hyperbole, metonymy, etc., within the overall context of straightforward narrative and didactic prose.[168]

Often the same event is recorded in two parallel accounts, with different details included. While this may present difficulty in harmonizing apparent contradictions, the variation itself does not necessitate a contradiction. "It is possible that if our knowledge were greater, all seeming difficulties could be swept away."[169] We should approach any difficult passage with the assumption that the writers knew more about the sub-

---

[168]Hanna, *Biblical Christianity*, 151-152.

[169]Harrison, "The Phenomena of Scripture," 250. See also Clarke, *Commentary*, 2:378 on errors by copiers.

ject than we know. Wesley acknowledged that difficulties exist in reconciling the genealogies of Matthew and Luke. He argued that both writers worked with the material to which they had access. "Nor was it needful they should correct the mistakes, if there were any."[170] But it should be noted that Wesley did not affirm that there were mistakes in the genealogies.

A different kind of issue stems from 1 Corinthians 7:6-12. In answer to the questions from Corinth, Paul speaks with apostolic authority in v 6. He is addressing a situation which had not been addressed in prior Scripture. But since all Scripture is profitable and Paul is writing Scripture, he is not simply giving an off-the-cuff opinion. However, in v 10, since Scripture has already addressed this issue, he cites precedent previously established in Matthew 5:32. However, in v 12 Paul speaks a new authoritative word to a new ethical question. Thus, the inspiration of Paul is equal to the inspiration of the rest of Scripture.

To carry this concept to a wider application, if *all* Scripture is from God and therefore authoritative, it does not matter whether the words are printed in red. We are to live by every word, regardless of color, that proceeds from the mouth of God (Matt 4:4).

---

[170]Wesley, *Notes*, 10.

Twenty Ways the Cults Misread the Bible

Paul warns of men who "handle the Word of God deceitfully" (2 Cor 4:2). Beware of "proof-texting" or reading into the passage your own presuppositions (eisogesis). This is called scripture twisting.[171]

1. Inaccurate quotation of Scripture. The founder of Transcendental Meditation quotes the words of Christ, "Be still and know that I am God" as an admonition for us all to recognize that we are God. Christ did not say these words; they are found in Psalm 46:10. More importantly, God is speaking and he alone is God.

2. Twisted translation. The *New World Translation* of Colossians 1:15-17 inserts the word *other* four times to change the meaning. This Jehovah's Witnesses translation of John 1:1 reads, "the Word was *a* god."

3. The Biblical hook. Cult propaganda is made to appear legitimate by a Scriptural quote which has no real con-

---

[171]This final section gleaned primarily from Sire, *Scripture Twisting*.

nection to what the cult asserts.

4. Ignoring the Immediate Context
    William J. Schnell, who was in the Jehovah's Witness organization for thirty years, wrote that in order to make people think they were studying the Bible, studies were conducted.

> The illusion created by looking up Scriptures here and there in the book study successfully obscured the fact that only 6½ percent of the Scriptures, and that in a disconnected way, were used in Watchtower books. Even this 6½ percent was feigned and weighted down with 93 ½ percent Watchtower verbiage.[172]

5. Collapsing Contexts. Two or more unrelated texts are treated as if they belong together. For example, Judas went out and hung himself. Go thou and do likewise. And what thou doest, do quickly!

6. Overspecification. Speculation on what is not specified

7. Word play. Adam can be divided into two syllables *a dam*. Sin became a dam or separation between man and God, according to Mary Baker Eddy. But this meaning cannot be sustained from the Hebrew.

8. Figurative fallacy. Mistaking literal language for figurative language or mistaking the figurative for the literal.

---

[172]Schnell, *Thirty Years A Watchtower Slave*, 124.

9. Speculative readings of predictive prophecy. Ezekiel 37:15-23 describes the coming together of two sticks. Mormonism teaches this is the joining together of the Bible and the book of Mormon.

10. Saying but Not Citing. Exotic writers sometimes claim the Bible teaches something, but do not give the reference. "God helps those who help themselves" is not in the Bible, but is often quoted.

11. Selective citing. Citing only references which appear to support your position without looking at all relevant passages. The *Scofield Reference Bible* states a proposition, followed by a long list of Scriptural citations. If you run these references they typically do not address the stated proposition.

12. Inadequate evidence. The citation of obscure references to support outlandish claims. A premature generalization is drawn from insufficient evidence. Joseph Smith was a high school dropout with a record of misdemeanor offences in New York. He certainly was not qualified to translate "Reformed Egyptian" tablets!

13. Confused definition. Ordinary biblical terms are given meanings foreign to their context. Supporters of reincarnation distort the biblical term "born again" in this way.

14. Ignoring alternative explanations. Jesus said, "I have other sheep" (John 10:16). *"Obviously,"* they say, "this proves there is life on other planets."

15. The obvious fallacy. The unfamiliar are overwhelmed

by the use of words like *obviously, undoubtedly, certainly, all scholars agree, etc.* This is given in the place of logical reasons.

16. Virtue by association. A cult writer quotes a respected Christian authority. For example, "Jesus is listed as one of the greatest gurus of all times." This is done to give credibility to all the other gurus listed. Sometimes cult writings adopt King James grammar in an attempt to sound more biblical.

17. Esoteric interpretation. Privileged information is claimed that a biblical passage has a certain meaning. No explanation is given for the interpretation other than this knowledge was imparted to the interpreter through the Spirit or an angel or a vision. I was told once that Ezekiel 16:6 stops bleeding.

18. Supplementing biblical authority. New revelation either replaces or is added to Scripture, such as the Book of Mormon or the Apocrypha. It is not legitimate to prove when Christ will return by the use of astrology or the study of pyramids.

19. Rejecting biblical authority. Interpreters either reject the Bible as a whole or a particular passage is rejected because it does not fit the interpreter's teachings.

20. World-view confusion. Scriptural statements, stories, commands, or symbols are lifted out of their context and given another frame of reference. "All things are yours"

(1 Cor 3:21) has been used as permission to steal![173]

Let the Word Control You

It is not enough to handle the Word of truth accurately. The Word must take hold of us and transform us. Martin Luther declared,

> Unless I am convinced by Scripture and clear reason — I do not accept the authority of popes and councils, for they have contradicted each other — my conscience is captive to the Word of God. I cannot and will not recant anything, for to go against conscience is neither right nor safe.[174]

Thus, we must live in the Word and biblical literature which explains Scripture. Wesley explained, "My ground is the Bible. Yea, I am a Bible-bigot. I follow it in all things, both great and small."[175] To those who claimed to have a better way, he demanded, "Show me it is so by

---

[173]Knapp, *Impressions*, 21.

[174]Bainton, *Here I Stand*, 144. *Clear* or *evident reason*, as Luther used the term meant a "logical inference from biblical principles" [Packer, "Sola Scriptura," 44].

[175]Wesley, *Journal*, 5 June 1766.

plain proof of Scripture."[176]

Wesley challenged his lay preachers to read and study. To those who had no taste for reading he replied, "Contract a taste for it by use, or return to your trade."[177]

In his *Address to the Clergy*, John Wesley considered what kind of men the clergy should be. Among the qualifications listed Wesley said:

> No less necessary is a knowledge of the Scriptures, which teach us how to teach others .... In order to do this accurately, ought he not to know the literal meaning of every word, verse, and chapter; without which there can be no firm foundation on which the spiritual meaning can be built? Should he not likewise be able to deduce the proper corollaries, speculative and practical, from each text; to solve the difficulties which arise, and answer the objections which are or may be raised against it; and to make a suitable application of all to the consciences of his hearers?
>
> But can he do this, in the most effectual manner, without a knowledge of the original tongues? Without this, will he not frequently be at a stand, even as to texts which regard practice only? But he will be under still greater difficulties, with respect to controverted scriptures. He will be ill able to rescue these out of the

---

[176]Wesley, *Preface* to Sermons, ¶ 9.

[177]Wesley, *BE Works*, 10:340. See similar advice to John Trembath in a letter written on 17 August 1760.

hands of any man of learning that would pervert them: For whenever an appeal is made to the original, his mouth is stopped at once.

Wesley continued by recommending a knowledge of history and especially the church fathers, the sciences, logic, philosophy, psychology, common sense, and personal refinement. Then he took inventory by asking, "Are we such, or are we not?"

Let us each seriously examine himself. Have I, (1.) Such a knowledge of Scripture, as becomes him who undertakes so to explain it to others, that it may be a light in all their paths? Have I a full and clear view of the analogy of faith, which is the clue to guide me through the whole? Am I acquainted with the several parts of Scripture; with all parts of the Old Testament and the New? Upon the mention of any text, do I know the context, and the parallel places? Have I that point at least of a good Divine, the being a good textuary? Do I know the grammatical construction of the four Gospels; of the Acts; of the Epistles; and am I a master of the spiritual sense (as well as the literal) of what I read? Do I understand the scope of each book, and how every part of it tends thereto? Have I skill to draw the natural inferences deducible from each text? Do I know the objections raised to them or from them.... Am I ready to give a satisfactory answer to each of these objections?
Do I understand Greek and Hebrew? Otherwise, how can I undertake, (as every Minister

does,) not only to explain books which are written therein, but to defend them against all opponents. Am I not at the mercy of every one who does understand, or even pretends to understand, the original? For which way can I confute his pretense? Do I understand the language of the Old Testament: critically? at all? Can I read into English one of David's Psalms; or even the first chapter of Genesis? Do I understand the language of the New Testament: Am I a critical master of it? Have I enough of it even to read into English the first chapter of St. Luke? If not, how many years did I spend at school? How many at the University? And what was I doing all those years? Ought not shame to cover my face?[178]

Wesley was not trying to intimidate. However, we cannot preach to others what we have not grasped. Adam Clarke urged preachers to "study yourself half to death and then pray yourself wholly to life."[179] These challenges from classic Methodism were not meant to convey that Bible study and preaching was best left to the professionals. In fact, they were issued to lay ministers who did not have formal theological training. My attempt with this book to show how to study Scripture is not aimed to curry favor within the academic guild. My goal is to help the busy bi-vocational pastor intentionally handle the Word more thoroughly and accurately.

---

[178]Wesley, *Works*, Jackson, ed. 10:480-491.

[179]Everett, *Adam Clarke Portrayed*, 2:362.

We work with words and we pray that God will use our words to prod and enlighten. We choose words carefully with the hope that the Holy Spirit will nail them down in the minds of those in our assembly until their life is changed (Eccl 12:11). The power is in the infallible Word, proclaimed by fallible ministers who are anointed by the same Holy Spirit who originally inspired the text. Yet in the divine-human effort, we must do the best we can to rightly handle the life-changing Word.

BIBLIOGRAPHY

Abott, Thomas Kingsmill. *A Critical and Exegetical Commentary on the Epistles to the Ephesians and to the Colossians: International Critical Commentary*. Edinburgh: T&T Clark, 1897.

Allis, Oswald T. "Modern Dispensationalism and the Doctrine of the Unity of Scripture." *The Evangelical Quarterly* 8:1 (15 January1936) 22-35.

Ames, William. *The Marrow of Theology*. 1643. John D. Eusden, ed. and transl. Reprint, Boston: Pilgrim, 1968.

Archer, Gleason L. "The Witness of the Bible to Its Own Inerrancy." *The Foundation of Biblical Authority*. James Montgomery Boice, ed. Grand Rapids: Zondervan, 1978.

__________. *Encyclopedia of Bible Difficulties*. Grand Rapids: Zondervan, 1982.

Augustine. *Reply to Faustus the Manichean. A Select Library of the Nicene and Post-Nicene Fathers of the Christian Church*. First Series. Vol. 4. Philip Schaff, ed. 1887. Reprint, Grand Rapids: Eerdmans, 1979 [*NPNF*]

__________. *Expositions on the Book of Psalms. A Select Library of the Nicene and Post-Nicene Fathers of the Christian Church*. First Series. Vol. 8. Philip Schaff, ed. 1888. Reprint, Grand Rapids: Eerdmans, 1979. [*NPNF*]

Baker, Frank. "John Wesley's Churchmanship." *London Quarterly and Holborn Review* 185 (October 1960) 269-274.

Bahnsen, Greg L. "The Inerrancy of the Autographa." *Inerrancy*. Norman L.Geisler, ed. Grand Rapids: Zondervan, 1979.

__________. *By This Standard: The Authority of God's Law Today*. Tyler, TX: Institute for Christian Economics, 1985.

Bainton, Roland H. *Here I Stand*. Nashville: Abingdon, 1950.

Barth, Karl. *Church Dogmatics*. 14 vols. G. W. Bromiley and T. F. Torrence, eds. Edinburgh: T&T Clark, 1932-1967.

Barton, John. *Reading the Old Testament: Method in Biblical Study*. Louisville: Westminster, 1984.

Bauer, David. *The Structure of Matthew's Gospel: A Study in Literary Design.* Sheffield: Almond Press, 1988.

Beale, Gregory K. *The Book of Revelation: The New International Greek Testament Commentary*. Grand Rapids: Eerdmans, 1999.

__________ and D. A. Carson. *Commentary on the New Testament Use of the Old Testament*. Grand Rapids: Baker, 2007.

Biel, Gabriel. *A Defense of Apostolic Obedience* 1, in *Defensorium Obedientiae Apostolicae et Alia Documenta*. Heiko A. Oberman, Daniel E. Zerfoss, and William J. Courtenay, eds. Cambridge: Harvard University Press, 1968.

Bloesch, Donald G. *Christian Foundations: Holy Scripture*. Downers Grove, IL: InterVarsity, 1994.

Brown, Francis, S. R. Driver, and Charles A. Briggs. *Hebrew and English Lexicon of the Old Testament*. Oxford: Clarendon, 1907. [*BDB*]

Brown, Ira. "Higher Criticism Comes to America," *Journal of the Presbyterian Historical Society* 38:4

(December 1960) 193-212.

Bornkamm, Heinrich. *Luther an the Old Testament*. Erich W and Ruth C. Gritch, transl. Philadelphia: Fortress, 1969.

Bultmann, Rudolf. "New Testament and Mythology." *Kergma and Myth*. H. W. Bartsch, ed. London: SPCK, 1957.

Burgon, John William. *Inspiration and Interpretation: Seven Sermons Preached before the University of Oxford*. London: J. H. and James Parker, 1861.

Callen, Barry L. and Richard P. Thompson, eds. *Reading the Bible in Wesleyan Ways*. Kansas City: Beacon Hill, 2004.

Calvin, John. *Calvin's Commentaries*. 22 vols. 1540-1565. Reprint, Grand Rapids: Baker, 1979.

Chapman, Alister. *Godly Ambition: John Stott and the Evangelical Movement*. New York: Oxford, 2012.

Chaves, Jonathan. "Soul and Reason: Deconstructing the Deconstructionists." *Journal of the American Oriental Society* 122:4 (October/December 2002) 828-835.

Chesterton, Gilbreth Keith. *Orthodoxy*. 1908. Reprint, Chicago: Moody, 2009.

Clarke, Adam. *Letter to a Preacher*. 1800. Reprint, *The Christian Prophet and His Work*. Salem, OH: Schmul, 1999.

__________. *The Holy Bible, Containing the Old and New Testaments: The Text Carefully Printed from the Most Correct Copies of the Present Authorized Translations, Including the Marginal reading and Parallel Tests; with a Commentary and Critical Notes, Designed as a help to a Better Understanding of the Sacred Writings*. 6 vols. 1811-1825. Reprint, Nashville: Abingdon, 1950.

Coleman, Robert E. *Nothing to Do But to Save Souls*. Grand Rapids: Francis Asbury Press, 1990.

Cooke, William. *Christian Theology*. 4th ed. London: Hamilton, Adams, & Company, 1863.

Corner, Daniel D. *A Critique of Gail Riplinger's Scholarship and KJV Onlyism*. Washington, PA: Evangelical Outreach, 1999.

Crenshaw, Curtis and Grover Gunn. *Dispensationalism Today, Yesterday, and Tomorrow*. Memphis: Footstool, 1985.

Currid, John. "A Cosmology of History From Creation to Consummation." *Building a Christian World View, II*. W. Andrew Hoffecker, ed. Philadelphia: Presbyterian & Reformed, 1987.

Custer, Stewart. *The Truth about the King James Version Controversy*. Greenville, SC: Bob Jones, 1981.

Dodd, C. H. *The Parables of the Kingdom*. Revised ed. London: James Nisbet, 1961.

Dunlap, Eldon Dale. "Methodist Theology in Great Britain." PhD diss, Yale University, 1956.

Earle, Ralph. "Matthew." *Beacon Bible Commentary*. Vol. 6. Kansas City: Beacon Hill, 1964.

Ehrman, Bart. *Misquoting Jesus: The Story Behind Who Changed the Bible and Why*. New York: HarperCollins, 2005.

Everett, James. *Adam Clarke Portrayed*. 2nd ed. London: W. Reed, 1866.

Farrar, F. W. *History of Interpretation*. Grand Rapids: Baker, 1961.

Fee, Gordon D. and Douglas Stuart. *How to Read the Bible for All Its Worth*. Grand Rapids: Zondervan, 1981.

Flew, Anthony. *Thinking Straight*. Buffalo: Prometheus, 1977.

Foxe, John. *Actes and Monuments of these Latter and Perillous Days, Touching Matters of the Church*. popularly known as *Foxe's Book of Martyrs*. London: John Day, 1563.

Frame, John M. *The Doctrine of the Knowledge of God*. Phillipsburg, NJ: Presbyterian & Reformed, 1987.

Fuhrman, Eldon R. "II Peter." Vol. 10. *Beacon Bible Commentary*. Kansas City: Beacon Hill, 1967. [*BBC*]

Gentry, Kenneth L. Jr.and Thomas Ice. *The Great Tribulation: Past or Future?* Grand Rapids: Kregel, 1999.

__________. "A Preterist View of Revelation." *Four Views on the Book of Revelation.* C. Marvin Pate, ed. Grand Rapids: Zondervan, 1998.

Glueck, Nelson. *Rivers in the Desert: A History of the Negev.* New York: Farrar, Strous and Cudahy, 1959.

Green, Joel B. *Reading Scripture as Wesleyans.* Nashville: Abingdon, 2010.

Gregg, Steve. *The Empire of the Risen Son: A Treatise on the Kingdom of God — What It Is and Why It Matters.* Book Two. *All the King's Men.* Maitland, FL: Xulon, 2020.

Hanegraaff, Hank. "Magic Apologetics." *Christian Research Journal* 20:1 (Sept-Oct 1997) 54-55.

Hanna, Mark M. *Biblical Christianity: Truth or Delusion?* Maitland, FL: Xulon, 2011.

__________. "Biblical Inerrancy Versus Midrashic Redactionism." Unpublished ETS paper, 1980.

Harrison, Everett F. "The Phenomena of Scripture." *Revelation and the Bible: Contemporary Evangelical Thought.* Carl F. H. Henry, ed. Grand Rapids: Baker, 1958.

Heiser, Michael. "Inspiration of Scripture Explained." https://www.youtube.com/watch?v=mKwtv0Zluvo

Henry, Carl F. H. *God, Revelation and Authority.* 6 vols. Waco: TX: Word, 1976-1983.

Hodge, A. A. and B. B. Warfield. "Inspiration." *Presbyterian Review* 2 (April 1881) 225-260.

Hodgkin, A. M. *Christ in All the Scriptures.* 1907. Reprint, Grand Rapids: Baker, 1976

Jordan, James B. *Through New Eyes.* Brentwood, TN: Wolgemuth & Hyatt, 1988.

Kaiser, Walter C. Jr. *Toward an Exegetical Theology.* Grand Rapids: Baker, 1981.

__________. "The Literary Form of Genesis 1-11."   *New*

Perspectives on the Old Testament. J. Barton Payne, ed. Waco, TX: Word, 1970.

Kantzer, Kenneth S. "Redaction Criticism: Is It Worth the Risk?" *Christianity Today* 29:15 (18 October 1985) 1-I to 12-I.

Kelly, Douglas F. *Systematic Theology*. 3 vols. Ross-shire, Scotland: Christian Focus, 2008-2021.

Knapp, Martin Wells. *Impressions*. Cincinnati: Revivalist, 1892.

Koskie, Steven J. "Wesleyan Hermeneutics." *Global Wesleyan Encyclopedia of Biblical Theology*. Robert D. Branson, ed. Kansas City: Beacon Hill, 2020.

Klein, William W, Craig L. Blomberg, and Robert L. Hubbard, Jr. *Introduction to Biblical Interpretation*. Revised. Nashville: Thomas Nelson, 2004.

Knox, John. *The History of the Reformation of Religion Within the Realm of Scotland*. 1559-1566. Reprint, Edinburgh: The Banner of Truth Trust, 1982.

Ladd, George Eldon. *New Testament and Criticism*. Grand Rapids: Eerdmans, 1967.

__________. "The Search for Perspective," *Interpretation*, 25 (January 1971) 451-462.

Lewis, C. S. *Fern-seed and Elephants and other Essays on Christianity*. London: Fontana, 1977.

Linnemann, Eta. *Biblical Criticism on Trial*. Robert Yarbrough, trans. Grand Rapids: Kregel, 2001.

__________. *Historical Criticism of the Bible*. Robert Yarbrough, trans. Grand Rapids: Kregel, 1990.

Luther, Martin. *The Bondage of the Will*. 1525. J. I. Packer and O. R. Johnston, eds. Westwood, NJ: Fleming H. Revell, 1957.

Lyons, George. "Hermeneutical Bases for Theology: Higher Criticism and the Wesleyan Interpreter." *Wesleyan Theological Journal* 18:1 (Spring 1983) 63-78.

MacArthur, John. *Revelation 1-11: The MacArthur New Testament Commentary*. Chicago: Moody, 1999.

MacRae, Allan A. and Robert C. Newman. *Facts on the*

Textus Receptus and the King James Version.
Hatfield, PA: Biblical School of Theology, 1975.

McAuliffe, Joseph R. "Everything is Broken." *Chalcedon Report* 366 (January 1996) 14-15.

Maier, Gerhard. *The End of the Historical-Critical Method*. Edward W. Leverenz and Rudolph F. Norden, trans. St. Louis: Concordia, 1977.

Moss, Richard Waddy. *The Rev. W. B. Pope, D. D.; Theologian and Saint*. London: Robert Culley, 1903.

Munhall, L. W. *Breakers! Methodism Adrift*. New York: Cook, 1913.

Noll, Mark A. *Between Faith and Criticism*. San Francisco: Harper & Row, 1986.

Oden, Thomas C. *John Wesley's Teachings*. 4 vols. Grand Rapids: Zondervan, 2012-2014.

__________. *Requiem*. Nashville: Abingdon, 1995.

Olsen, V. Norskov. "The Christ Alone: The Christomonistic Principle." *Ministry* 53:2 (January 1980) 4-8.

Olson Roger E. "Back to the Bible (Almost)." *Christianity Today* 40:6 (20 May, 1996) 31-34.

Packer, James I. "Infallible Scripture and the Role of Hermeneutics." *Scripture and Truth*. D. A. Carson and John D. Woodbridge, eds. Grand Rapids: Baker, 1983.

__________. "Hermeneutics and Biblical Authority." *Themelios* 1:1 (Autumn 1975) 3-12.

__________. "Biblical Authority, Hermeneutics and Inerrancy." *Jerusalem and Athens*. E. R. Geehan, ed. Nutley, NJ: Presbyterian & Reformed, 1971.

__________. *"Fundamentalism" and the Word of God*. Grand Rapids: Eerdmans, 1958.

Panosian, Edward M. *What is the "Inspired" Word of God?* Greenville, SC: Bob Jones University, 1979.

Pinnock, Clark H. *Biblical Revelation*. Chicago: Moody, 1971.

Pope, William Burt. *A Compendium of Christian Theology*. 3 vols. London: Wesleyan Conference Office, 1880.

Radmacher, Earl D. and Robert D. Preus, eds.
    Hermeneutics, Inerrancy, and the Bible. Grand
    Rapids: Zondervan, 1984.
Ramm, Barnard. *Protestant Biblical Interpretation*. 3rd
    ed. Grand Rapids: Baker, 1970.
__________. *After Fundamentalism: The Future of
    Evangelical Theology*. New York: Harper & Row, 1982.
Reasoner, Vic. "Karl Barth's Dialectic Doublespeak." *The
Arminian Magazine* 41:2 (Fall 2023) 1-5.
__________. *The Importance of Inerrancy*. Evansville: IN:
    Fundamental Wesleyan, 2013.
__________. "Hidden Prophecies in the Psalms?" *The
    Church Herald and Holiness Banner* (7 May 1988) 6.
Rice, John R. *Our God-Breathed Book – The Bible*.
Murfreesboro, TN: Sword of the Lord, 1969.
Rittgers, Ronald K. ed. *Hebrews, James*. Vol. 13 of
    Reformation Commentary on Scripture. Downers
    Grove, IL: InterVarsity, 2017. [*RCS*]
Rosscup, James E. "Hermeneutics." Unpublished course
    syllabus, 1977.
Rushdoony, Rousas John. *The Institutes of Biblical Law*.
    Nutley, NJ: Presbyterian & Reformed, 1973.
Schaff, Philip. *History of the Christian Church*. 8 vols. 5th
    ed. 1889. Reprint, Grand Rapids: Eerdmans, 1980.
Schnell, William J. *Thirty Years A Watchtower Slave*.
    Grand Rapids: Baker, 1971.
Scofield, Cyrus Ingersoll. *Rightly Dividing the Word of
    Truth*. Grand Rapids: Zondervan, 1936.
Showers, Renand E. *There Really Is a Difference: A
    Comparison of Covenant and Dispensational
    Theology*. Bellmawr, NJ: Friends of Israel Gospel
    Ministry, 1990.
Sire, James W. *Scripture Twisting*. Downers Grove, IL:
    InterVarsity, 1980.
Spong, John Shelby. *Biblical Literalism: A Gentile Heresy*.
    New York: HarperCollins, 2017.
Sproul, R. C. "A Journey Back in Time." *Tabletalk* 23:1

(January 1999) 7.

Steele, Daniel. *Half-Hours with St. John's Epistles*. 1901. Reprint, Salem, OH: Schmul, 1972.

Stevens, Abel. *The Life and Times of Nathan Bangs*. New York: Carlton & Porter, 1863.

Stott, John R. W. *Baptism and Fullness*. 2nd ed. Downers Grove, IL: InterVarsity, 1976. The first edition was entitled *The Baptism and Fullness of the Holy Spirit* (1964).

Stuart, Douglas. "Interpret = Understand + Explain," *Decision Magazine* 36:4 (April 1995) 11-12.

Summers, Ray. *Worthy is the Lamb*. Nashville: Broadman, 1951.

Summers, Thomas O. *Systematic Theology*. 2 vols. John Tigert, ed. Nashville: Methodist Episcopal Church, South, 1888.

Tenney, Merrill C. *Interpreting Revelation*. Grand Rapids: Eerdmans, 1957.

Terry, Milton S. *Biblical Hermeneutics*. 2nd ed. 1885. Reprint, Grand Rapids: Zondervan, 1974.

Tertullian, *The Prescription Against Heretics. The Ante-Nicene Fathers*. Vol. 3. Alexander Roberts and James Donaldson, eds. 1885. Reprint, Grand Rapids: Eerdmans, 1978. [*ANF*]

Thomas, Robert L. *Introduction to Exegesis*. Unpublished, 1981.

Thorsen, Donald A. D. *The Wesleyan Quadrilateral*. Grand Rapids: Francis Asbury, 1990.

Turner, George Allen. "John Wesley as an Interpreter of Scripture." *Inspiration and Interpretation*. John Walvoord, ed. Grand Rapids: Eerdmans, 1957.

Wallace, Daniel B. "Did the Original New Testament Manuscripts still exist in the Second Century?" http://bible.org/article/did-original-new-testament-manuscripts-still-exist-second-century

Wesley, John. *The Bicentennial Edition of the Works of John Wesley*. 35 vols. when complete; 26 volumes to

date. Randy Maddox, ed. Nashville: Abingdon, 1976-.
[*BE*]

__________. *The Works of John Wesley*. Thomas Jackson, ed. Third edition. 14 vols. 1872. Reprint, Grand Rapids: Zondervan, 1979.

__________. *Explanatory Notes Upon the Old Testament*. 3 vols. 1765. Reprint, Salem, OH: Schmul. 1975.

Wiley, H. Orton. *Christian Theology*. Kansas City: Beacon Hill, 1940-1943.

Wisdom, Thurman. "Textus Receptus: Is it Fundamental to Our Faith?" *Faith for the Family* (October 1979) 3-4.

Wood, A. Skevington. *The Burning Heart*. Minneapolis: Bethany, 1967.

__________. *Captive to the Word : Martin Luther, Doctor of Sacred Scripture*. Grand Rapids: Eerdmans, 1969.

Wood, Charles R. "The Question of Preservation." *Faith for the Family* (November 1981) 13-14.

Wynkoop, Mildred Bangs. "A Hermeneutical Approach to John Wesley."*Wesleyan Theological Journal* 6:1 (Spring 1971) 13-22.

Young, Edward J. *In the Beginning: Genesis Chapters 1 to 3 and the Authority of Scripture*. Edinburgh: Banner of Truth, 1976.